Hot-Water Bottle Covers

Hot-Water Bottle Covers

CHRISSIE DAY

GUILD OF MASTER
CRAFTSMAN PUBLICATIONS

First published 2008 by
Guild of Master Craftsman Publications Ltd
Castle Place, 166 High Street,
Lewes, East Sussex BN7 1XU

Reprinted 2010

Text and Designs © Chrissie Day, 2008
© In the Work, GMC Publications Ltd, 2008

Copyright details: Chrissie Day 2008-04-01
The right of Chrissie Day to be identified as the author
of this work has been asserted in accordance with the
Copyright, Designs and Patents Act 1988, sections 77
and 78.

ISBN: 978-1-86108-617-4

A catalogue record of this book is available from
the British Library.

Knitting and crochet illustrations by Simon Rodway

Associate Publisher: Jonathan Bailey
Managing Editor: Gerrie Purcell
Production Manager: Jim Bulley
Editor: Alison Howard
Managing Art Editor: Gilda Pacitti
Design & Photography: Rebecca Mothersole

Set in Gill Sans and Ribbon

Colour origination by GMC Reprographics
Printed and bound by KNP, Thailand

Why we love hot-water bottle covers

Cozy

Old technology is often the best, and there is nothing more warming
and comforting than snuggling down with a hot-water bottle.
Add a hand-knitted cover in beautiful yarn and your cold toes
will feel the benefit for years to come.

There is a cover in this book for every member of the family, from the
newest baby to the most macho man of the house.
Give them as gifts or cheer yourself up on a cold winter night
by making one for yourself.

Snuggle and enjoy.

Contents

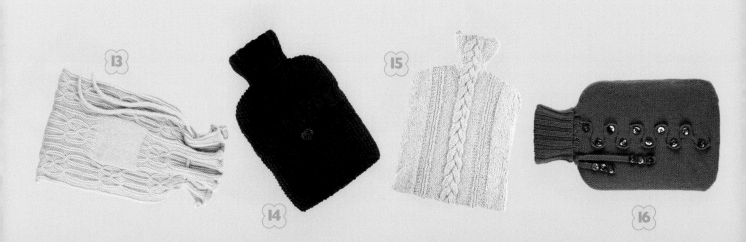

This cover is ideal for a winter baby's crib.
It's made in soft pastel stripes,
and the soft cotton yarn will not tickle tiny toes.

Baby Cotton

Materials

- Filatura di Crosa Porto Cervo
  (88yds/80m per 50g ball)
- 1 x 50 ball shade 65 Olive
- 1 x 50g ball shade 33 Red
- 1 x 50g ball shade 30 Yellow
- 1 x 50g ball shade 28 Blue
- A pair of 3.75mm (UK9:US5) needles

Measurements

5½in (14cm) wide x 7in (18cm) long to shoulder
of cover

Tension

20 sts x 28 rows to 4in (10cm) over stocking stitch using
3.75mm needles

Special techniques

Main body of cover is worked in stocking stitch, joining in
colours as necessary for stripes

Front

Cast on 18 sts and work in st st foll the 26-row stripe sequence (below).

Stripe sequence

Blue	10 rows
Olive	4 rows
Red	4 rows
Yellow	4 rows
Blue	2 rows
Red	2 rows
Olive	2 rows
Yellow	4 rows
Olive	2 rows
Blue	6 rows
Yellow	6 rows

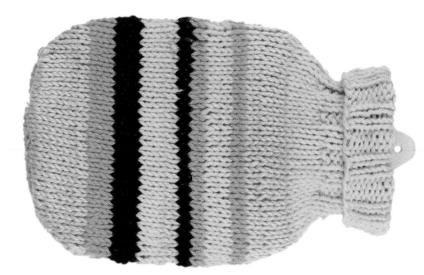

Row 1 (RS): K all sts.
Cast on 2 sts at beg of next 2 rows.
Inc1 at each end of next and foll 2 alt rows (28 sts).
Work straight until cover measures 6in (15cm), ending with RS facing.
Dec 1 st at each end of next and foll 2 alt rows.
Purl 1 row.
Cast off 2 sts at beg of next 2 rows (18 sts).
Leave rem sts on a spare length of yarn.

Back

Work as for front but leave sts on needle (18 sts)
Still using 3.75mm needles, with RS of cover facing, and working in k2, p2 rib, foll the rib stripe sequence.

Rib stripe sequence

Yellow	8 rows
Olive	2 rows
Yellow	10 rows

Row 1 (RS): K1, *p2, k2; rep across the 18 sts, ending with p1. Transfer sts left on spare yarn to left needle and work p1, *k2, p2; rep from * to last st, k1.
Row 2: P1, *k2, p2; rep from * to last 3 sts, k2, p1.
Row 3: K1, *p2, k2; rep from * to last 3 sts, p2, k1.
Rep last 2 rows until rib measures 4in (10cm).
Cast off in rib.

Making up

Press lightly, foll directions on ball band.
Join side and bottom seams.
Join collar seam reversing half-way to allow it to be folded over.
Place bottle in cover by folding and inserting through collar.

This snugly cover is ideal for a toddler's first bed.
The yarn comes in a range of shades, so vary the stripes
to match the nursery.

Toddler Stripe

Materials

- Filatura di Crosa Zarella (120 yds/110m per 50g ball)
- 1 x 50g ball shade 2 Green (M)
- 1 x 50g ball shade 11 Cream (C)
- A pair of 3.75mm (UK9:US5) needles

Tension

20 sts x 28 rows to 4in (10cm) over stocking stitch using
3.75mm needles

Measurements

5½in (14 cm) wide x 7in (18cm) long to shoulder
of cover

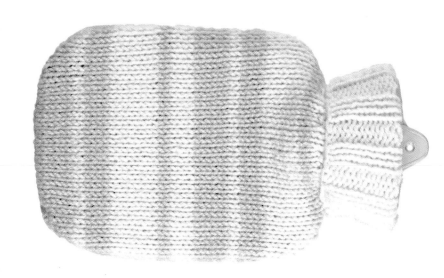

Back

Work as for front until*.

Leave rem sts on needle (18 sts).

Next row (RS): Using C only, K1, *p2, k2; rep across the 18 sts ending with p1. Transfer sts left on spare length of yarn to left needle.

Next row: P1, *k2, p2; rep from * to last st, k1.

Next row: P1, *k2, p2; rep from * to last 3 sts, k2, p1.

Next row: K1, *p2, k2; rep from * to last 3 sts, p2, k1.

Rep last 2 rows till ribbing measures 4in (10cm).

Cast off in rib.

Front

Using M and 3.75mm needles, cast on 18 sts and work in st st throughout.

Row 1 (RS): Following the stripe sequence below, k to end.

Cast on 2 sts at the beg of next 2 rows (22 sts).

Inc 1 st at each end of next and foll 2 alt rows (28 sts).

Work straight till cover measures 6in(15cm), ending with RS facing for next row.

Dec 1 st at each end of next and foll 2 alt rows.

Purl 1 row.

Cast off 2 sts at beg of next 2 rows.*

Leave rem sts on a spare length of yarn.

Stripe sequence

Col M 6 rows
Col C 2 rows
Col M 4 rows
Col C 8 rows
Col M 2 rows
Col C 4 rows

Rep these 26 rows throughout.

Making up

Press carefully, foll instructions on ball band.

Join side and bottom seams.

Join collar seam, reversing seam halfway up collar to allow for it to be folded over.

Insert hot water bottle by folding it and placing it through the polo neck.

Toddler Stripe

This fun cover is made from a luxurious loop effect mohair yarn that looks just like teddy bear fur. Buttons make its nose and eyes.

Teddy Toes

Materials
- Knitglobal Superkid Loop Mohair chunky (109yds/100m per 100g hank)
- 1 × 100g hank Walnut
- A pair of 5mm (UK6:US8) needles
- A 5mm (UK6:US8) circular needle
- 3 × 1in (5cm) buttons

Measurements
13 × 9in (33 × 23cm) unstretched – to fit standard size hot water bottle

Tension
Not critical as cover is stretchy

Special techniques
- Circular knitting
- Garter stitch in the round (k one round, p one round)

Neck

Cast on 37 stitches.

Work 4 rows g-st.

Row 5: K2tog, k16, place marker, k2tog, k17.

Row 6: K2tog, k15, place marker, k2tog, k16.

Cont as set, dec at beg of row and after marker, until 25 sts rem.

Work 3 rows g-st.

Next row (inc for shoulders): K2, inc, k to marker, inc, k to end.

Rep last row until there are 57 sts on needle.

Body

Transfer work to circular needle and join into a circle.

Work g-st in the round until cover measures 9in (23cm) or length desired to fit bottle.

Next round: Cast off 31 sts, work to end.

Flap

Work straight in g-st for 2in (5cm).

Next row (single buttonhole): K12, cast off 2 sts, k12,

Next row: K12, cast on 2 sts, k12.

Work straight in g-st for 2in (5cm).

Next row (two buttonholes): K7, cast off 2 sts, k8, cast off 2 sts, k7.

Next row: K7, cast on 2 sts, k8, cast on 2 sts, k7.

Work 2 rows g-st.

Cast off.

Making up

Sew up side of funnel neck.

Attach buttons to correspond with buttonholes.

Tip

If you really want to enhance the 'teddy effect', substitute a plastic nose and eyes for the buttons. You will find these in good haberdashery stores.

This clever space-dyed yarn forms an intricate pattern
before your very eyes! Made from acrylic, it is ideal
for anyone who is allergic to wool.

Greek Isles

Materials

- Elle Escapade DK (300yds/275m per 100g ball)
- 1 x 100g ball 75003 Swinging
- A 4mm (UK8:US6) circular knitting needle
- Two short 4mm (UK8:US6) double-pointed needles
  for cord

Measurements

9in (23cm) wide x 14½in (37cm) long including top
gathering

Tension

22 sts x 30 rows to 4in (10cm) over stocking stitch using
4mm needles

Special techniques

- Circular knitting (see techniques section)
- Stocking stitch in the round = every row knit
- I-cord for drawstring (see overleaf)

Note: lengths of yarn may be selected to obtain the desired colour effect. In the example, the first few rows of the cord were worked in dark turquoise to produce a contrast centre for the large pinwheel. At the other end, one of the narrow cords was worked in pale turquoise with a deep turquoise centre, and the other in deep turquoise with the final 10 rows in pale turquoise.

Making up

Fold over top to create picot edge and catch stitch down.

Pin cover out to size and damp-press foll instructions on ball band.

Join bottom edge using mattress stitch.

Back and front

Cast on 100 sts.

Work 70 rounds st st.

Round 71: *k2, yrn, k2tog, k4; rep from * to last 4 sts, yrn, k2tog, k2.

Work 2 rounds.

Round 74: *k2, k2tog, k4; rep from * to end (77 sts).

Work 20 rounds knit.

Cast off k-wise.

Drawstring

Using 4mm double-pointed needles cast on 6 sts.

Next row: K6 but do not turn; slide sts to other end of needle, draw yarn up tightly behind sts and k6 again.

Rep last row until cord will go through eyelets when cover is laid flat, plus about 30 rows for large pinwheel.

Next row: Divide the 6 sts and work 2 cords of 3 sts each and 30 rows long for the small pinwheels.

Roll up the ends of the cord to make pinwheels as shown and sew in place.

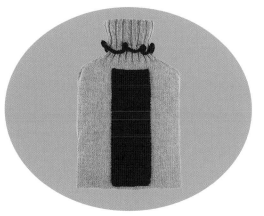

This simple cover is made special with a tantalizing lace panel
that is sewn on afterwards. The stretch 'polo neck'
allows easy bottle insertion.

Lacy Nights

Materials

- Filatura di Crosa Zarina Merino Extra Fine
  (181yds/165m per 50g ball)
- 2 × 50g balls shade 1494 grey (M)
- Elle Stretch DK (170yds/155m per 50g ball)
- 1 × 50g ball shade 017 black (C)
- A pair of 3mm (UK11:US2–3) needles
- A pair of 3.25mm (UK10:US3) needles
- A pair of 3.75mm (UK9:US5) needles
- 2 large buttons
- Black sewing thread

Measurements

9in (23cm) wide × 14½in (37cm) long including collar

Tension

28 sts × 36 rows to 4in (10cm) over stocking stitch using
M and 3.25mm needles

Special techniques

- M1 = make 1 by lifting horizontal thread between stitch
  just worked and foll st and knitting into the back of it.

Cover

Using 3mm needles and M, cast on 66 sts.

Row 1 (RS): *k2, p2, rep from * to last 2 sts, k2.

Row 2: *p2, k2, rep from * to last 2 sts, p2.

Rep these 2 rows 3 times (8 rows).

Change to 3.25mm needles.

With RS facing and beg with a knit row, dec 2 sts across first row.

Next row: P all sts.

Cont in st st until cover measures 4in (10cm) from cast-on edge.

Place a marker at each end of row for lower back fold.

Cont in st st until cover measures 14½in (37cm), ending with RS facing

Top neck shaping

Next 4 rows: Dec 1 st at each end.

Next 2 rows: Cast off 4 sts at beg, work to end.

Next 2 rows: Cast off 3 sts at beg, work to end.

Next 3 rows: Dec 1 st at each end.

Purl 1 row.

Leave rem 36 sts on a spare length of yarn.

Upper back

Using 3mm needles, cast on 66 sts

Row 1: *k2, p2, rep from * to last 2 sts, k2.

Row 2: *p2, k2, rep from * to last 2 sts, p2.

Rep row 1 once more.

Next row (buttonhole): Rib 20, cast off 3 sts, rib 19, cast off 3 sts, rib 19.

Next row: Work in rib as set, cast on 3 sts over each set of cast-off sts.

Work 3 rows rib.

Change to 3.25mm needles.

Next row (RS): K all sts, dec 2 sts evenly across row.

Next row: P to end.

Cont in st st until back measures 7½in (19cm) from cast-on edge.

Top neck shaping

Work as for front.

Top ribbing

Row 1 (RS): *k2, p1, rep from * to end (36 sts) but do not turn.

Place 36 sts from spare yarn on left needle and work row 1 again across these sts so there are 72 sts on right needle, turn.

Change to 3mm needles

Rep row 1 until rib collar measures 6¾in (17cm), ending with RS facing for next row.

Change to contrast yarn.

Next row: P to end.

Next row: *k1, m1, rep from * to last st, k1.

Next row: P to end.

Next row: K to end.

Cast off p-wise.

Lace panel

Using 3.75mm needles and the thumb method, cast on 21 sts in C.

Work 2 rows g-st.

Pattern

Row 1 (RS): K5, (yf, sl1, k1, psso) twice, k3, (k2tog, yf) twice, k5.

Row 2 and every alt row (WS): K2, p to last 2 sts, k2 (wrong side).

Row 3: K6, (yf, SL1, k1, psso) twice, k1 (k2tog, yf) twice, k6.

Row 5: K7, yf, Sl1, k1, psso, yf, sl1, k2tog, psso, yf, k2tog, yf, k7.

Row 7: K8, yf, sl1, k2tog, psso, yf, k2tog, yf, k8.

Row 9: K8, (k2tog, yf) twice, k9.

Row 11: K7, (k2tog, yf) twice, k1, yf, sl1, k1, psso, k7.

Row 13: K6, (k2tog, yf) twice, k1, (yf, sl1, k1, psso) twice, k6.

Row 15: K5, (k2tog, yf) twice, k3, (yf, sl1, k1, psso) twice, k5.

Row 17: K4, (k2tog, yf) twice, k5, (yf, sl1, k1, psso) twice, k4.

Row 18: K2, p to last 2 sts, k2.

Rep these 18 rows 4 times more ending with RS facing for next row.

Next row: K2, p17, k2.

Next row: P to end.

Cast off p-wise.

Making up

Starting from lower edge markers, place panel in the centre of cover ending at top neck shaping and sew in place using black cotton thread.

Fold cover at markers and join lower front and lower back seams.

Join top front and back seams, overlapping rib of top over rib of lower back to form flap.

Join collar seams and fold rib collar over to form a polo neck.

Attach buttons as shown.

This easy cover is given a special touch: simple bows made from contrasting strips of garter stitch are threaded through eyelets in the body.

Jaunty Bows

Materials

- Rowan Wool Cotton (124yds/113m per 50g ball)
- 2 x 50g balls shade 930 green (M)
- 2 x 50g balls shade 943 pink (C)
- A pair of 3.25mm (UK10:US3) needles
- A pair of 3.75mm (UK9:US5) needles
- A 3.50mm (UK9:USE/4) crochet hook

Measurements

9in (23cm) wide x 15in (38cm) long including top gathering

Tension

24 sts x 32 rows to 4in (10cm) over stocking stitch using 3.75mm needles

Special techniques

- The cover is worked in stocking stitch throughout

Side A

Using 3.75mm needles and M cast on
30 sts.

Knit 1 row.

Cast on 4 sts at beg of next 4 rows.

Inc1 at each end of next 2 rows.

Inc1 at each end of foll 2 alt rows.

Next row (WS): P to end.

Cont in st st until cover measures
3in (7.5cm), ending with RS facing for
next row.

Next row (bow eyelets): K18, ssk, yo,
k3, yo, k2tog, k to end.

Cont in st st until cover measures 6in
(15.5cm) ending with RS facing.

Next row (bow eyelets): K18, ssk, yo,
k3, yo, k2tog, k to end.

Cont in st st until cover measures 9in
(23cm) ending with RS facing.

Next row (bow eyelets): K21, ssk, yo,
k3, yo, k2tog, k to end.

Cont in st st until cover measures 12in
(30cm) ending with RS facing.

Neck eyelets

Next row: K6, *k2tog, yo, k6, rep from
* to end (6 eyelets made).

Cont in st st until cover measures 14½in
(37cm) ending with RS facing.

Change to 3.25mm needles and k 3 rows.

Cast off k-wise.

Side B

Work as for side A but use yarn C
throughout.

Bows

Using 3.25mm needles and the thumb
method, cast on 3 sts.

Work in g-st (every row k) until bow
measures 14in (36cm).

Cast off k-wise.

Make 3 bows in M and 3 in C.

Making up

Pin out and damp press the two
main pieces.

Join sides and bottom edge leaving
top open.

Thread contrasting lengths of g-st
through the pairs of eyelets on each side
of the cover and tie in bows.

Drawstring

Using 3.50mm crochet hook and one
strand each of M and C, make a chain
26in (66cm) long.

Fasten off.

Sew in ends and thread through the top
row of eyelets, starting and ending at side
edge of cover.

Place bottle in cover, pull the drawstring
tight and tie into a bow.

Variegated chenille yarn in the soft lilac tones
of an English garden lifts this
vintage-feel design into this century.

Chenille Chic

Materials

- Araucania Quellon viscose/rayon (99yds/90m per 100g ball)
- 2 x 100g balls
- A pair of 4mm (UK8:US6) needles
- A pair of 5mm (UK6:US8) needles
- 5 buttons

Measurements

8in wide x 14½in (37cm) long including top shaping

Tension

16 sts x 32 rows to 4in (10cm) over garter stitch using 4mm needles

Rep rows 8 and 9 twice more.
Change to 4mm needles.
Row 14: *p2tog, rep from * to end
of row.
Cont in patt until 5 repeats have
been worked

Top neck shaping

Change to 5mm needles.**
Next row: K to end.
Next 5 rows: K2 tog tbl, k to last
2 sts, k2tog.
Next 8 rows: Foll patt rows 7–14.
Cont in patt as set until 3 repeats
have been worked from ** ending
with row 14.
Next row (RS): K to end.
Next 5 rows: Inc1, k to last st, inc1.
Next 8 rows: Follow patt from row 7.
Work 10 more rows ending with RS
facing for next row.
Next row (buttonhole): K5, *cast off
2 sts, k8, rep from * once more, cast
off 2 sts, k4.
Next row: Knit, casting on 2 sts over
cast-off sts on previous row.
Work 3 more rows g-st.
Cast off k-wise using 5mm needles.

Lower back

Work as for front, changing needles as
set, until 4 patt reps have been worked,
ending with RS facing for next row.
Work 7 rows g-st.
Cast off k-wise using 5mm needles.

Front and upper back

Using 5mm needles and the thumb
method cast on 32 sts.
Change to 4mm needles (RS facing
for next row).

Stitch pattern

Work 6 rows g-st.
Row 7: M1 along the row by working
into the front and back of each st
(64 sts).
Change to 5mm needles.
Row 8: P to end.
Row 9: K to end.

Making up

Join lower back to lower front, matching
lines on patt.
Fold over front top neck shaping to top
back shaping and sew in place,
overlapping the last g-st stripe for the
buttonhole flap.
Attach buttons to correspond to
buttonholes.

This unique hand-spun silk yarn needs only a simple pattern to make it absolutely stunning.

Brilliant Boxes

Materials

- Teo handspun handyed silk (length varies as yarn is handspun)
- Approximately 125g
- 1 pair of 4mm (UK8:US6) needles
- 1yd (1m) toning velvet ribbon

Measurements

9in (23cm) wide x 13in (33cm) long including top gathering (adjustable)

Tension

20 sts x 24 rows to 4in (10cm) over st st using 4mm needles

Special techniques

- Yrn (yarn round needle) = bring yarn forward and wrap round needle once

Adjust length here if necessary by working one more rep of patt.

Next row (eyelets): Keeping the box sequence as set, *k3, yrn, k2tog, rep from * to last 3 sts, yrn, k2tog, k1.

Work 6 rows k2, p2 rib.

Cast off.

Back

Cast on 33 sts.

Next row: (k3, p7) 3 times, k3.

Next row: (p3, k7) 3 times, p3.

Rep last two rows 3 times more.

Next row: P3, (k7, p3) 3 times.

Next row: K3, (p7, k3) 3 times.

Rep last 2 rows 3 times more.

Next row (eyelets, RS facing):
Keeping the box sequence as set,
*k3, yrn, k2tog, rep from * to last 3 sts,
yrn, k2tog, k1.

Work 6 rows k2, p2 rib.

Making up

Join seams.

Do not block or wet press.

Thread length of matching ribbon through eyelets and tie in a bow.

Front

Using 4mm needles, cast on 33 sts.

Next row (RS): (P3, k7) 3 times, p3.

Next row (WS): (k3, p7) 3 times, k3.

Rep last 2 rows 3 times more.

Row 9: K3, (p7, k3) 3 times.

Row 10: P3, (k7, p3) 3 times.

Rep last 2 rows 3 times more.

Rep the 2 blocks of design in order 3 times.

Work rows 1–8 once more.

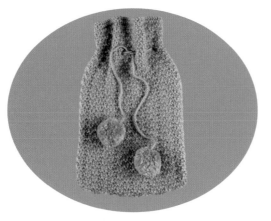

This cover is made in a simple but effective double seed stitch pattern in softest alpaca. Pompons complete its old-fashioned charm.

Super Seeds

Materials

- Debbie Bliss Alpaca Silk (71yds/65m per 50g ball)
- 4 x 50g balls shade 17 Light Teal
- A pair of 4.50mm (UK7:US7) needles
- A pair of 4mm (UK8:US6) needles
- Plastic template for pompons or cardboard for template.

Measurements

9in (23cm) wide x 14½in (37cm) long including top frill

Tension

18 sts x 24 rows to 4in (10cm) over stocking stitch using 4.50mm needles
17 sts and 22 rows to 4in (10cm) over stocking stitch using 4.50mm needles

Special techniques

- M1 = work into front and back of st to make 1 extra st
- Pompons – see techniques section

Back and front (make 2 alike)

Using 4.50mm needles, cast on 4 sts.

Row 1: K2, p2.

Row 2: M1, p to last st, M1 (6 sts).

Row 3: M1, p3, k1, m1 (8 sts).

Row 4: As row 2 (10 sts).

Row 5: M1, p2, k2, p3, k1, M1 (12 sts).

Row 6: As row 2 (14 sts).

Row 7: Cast on 10 sts at beg of row, (p3, k2) 4 times, p3, k1 (24 sts).

Row 8: Cast on 10 sts at beg of row, p to end (34 sts).

Row 9: M1, k1, (p3, k2) 6 times, p1, M1 (36 sts).

Row 10: As row 1 (38 sts).

Row 11: M1, k1, (p3, k2) 7 times, M1 (40 sts).

Row 12: P to end.

Row 13: * p3, k2, rep from * to end

Row 14: P to end.

Row 15: * p3, k2, rep from * to end.

Row 16: P to end

Row 17: *p1, k2, p2; rep from * to end.

Rep last 4 rows until cover measures 11½in (29cm) from row 8.

End with RS facing for next row.

Eyelet Row

Next row (RS): *(patt 4, k2tog, yf) rep from * to last 4 sts, patt 4.

Next row: P all sts.

Cont in patt as set until cover measures 14in (35.5cm) from row 8, ending with RS facing for next row.

Change to 4mm needles and work 3 rows g-st.

Cast off k-wise.

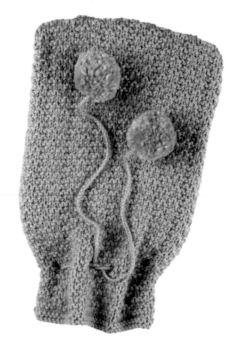

Making up

Dry press with a cool iron.

Join sides and bottom seam leaving top open.

Cord

Using three lengths of yarn, make a plait 34in (86cm) long.

Note: allow at least 4 times the length required for each plait, plus about 4in (10cm) each end to tie the pompons.

Beg and ending at centre front, thread plait through eyelets.

Pompons

Using a ready-made template or 2 × 2in (5cm) card circles with a smaller circle cut in the middle, wind yarn round until central hole is filled. Insert narrow-pointed scissors between halves of template and cut yarn carefully all round. Part halves of template and tie into centre of pompon using spare yarn at end of cord. Pull tightly and knot. Ease off template and fluff up pompon. Trim surface to form a smooth ball. Make second pompon and tie to other end of cord.

Insert bottle in cover, pull plait to fit neck and tie in a bow.

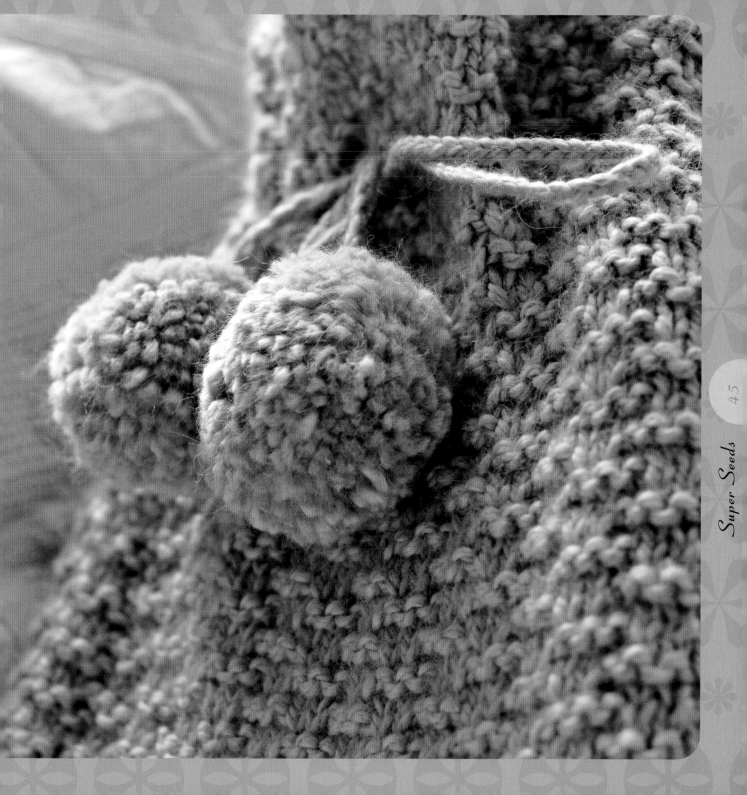

This snug felted cover is really easy to make with yarn that is specially designed for felting. It also looks good in midnight blue.

Starry Night

Materials

- Zitron Loft Color (110yds/101m per 50g ball)
- 3 x 50g balls 535 black
- 1 ball silver thread
- 6.5mm (UK3:US10.5) circular needle
- Narrow ribbon

Measurements

Felted to fit bottle

Tension

Not critical as work is felted

Special techniques

- Felting

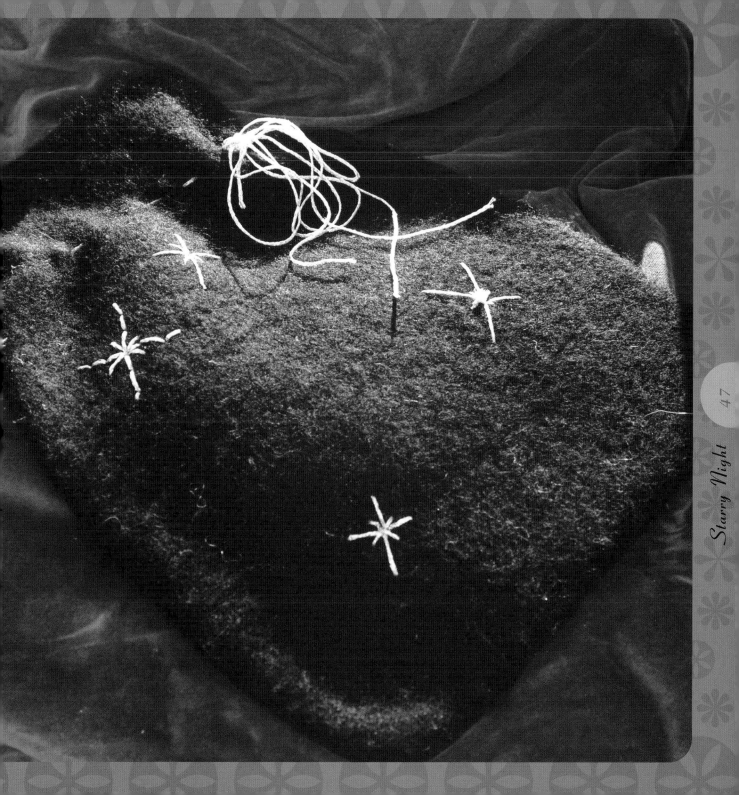

Cover

Using 6.5mm needle, cast on 90 sts.
Work in rounds of stocking stitch until
work measures 16in (40cm)
Next round: (K1, k2tog), rep to end
(60 sts).
Work 2 rounds st st.
Next round (eyelets): *ssk, k1,
yo, rep from * to end.
Work 23 rounds st st.
Purl 2 rounds.
Fasten off.

Making up

Join bottom edge.
Felt following instructions on ball band.
After felting place bottle in cover and
pull to fit.
Leave to dry.
Thread satin ribbon through eyelets.
Embroider stars on cover as show using
silver thread.

The hearts on this lovely green felted cover are cut from separately-worked felted fabric and applied wherever takes your fancy. Gorgeous!

Heart Felt

Materials

- Zitron Loft Color (110yds/101m per 50g ball)
- 3 x 50g balls dark green (M)
- 1 x 50g ball pink (A)
- 1 x 50g ball raspberry (B)
- A 6.5mm (UK3:US10.5) circular needle

Measurements

Felted to fit bottle

Tension

Not critical as work is felted

Special techniques

- Felting

Fabric for hearts

Using A, cast on 50 sts.
Work in g-st (every row k) for 25 rows.
Join in B and begin to work in stripes
alternating 1 row A, 1 row B.
Cont in B only for a further 25 rows.
Cast off.

Cover

Using 6.5mm circular needle cast on
90 sts.
Work in rounds of st st (every row k)
until work measures 16in (40.5cm).
Next round (dec): (k1, k2tog), rep
to end (60 sts).
Work 26 rounds st st.
Next 2 rounds: P to end.
Cast off.

Making up

Join bottom edge of cover.
Felt cover and fabric according to
instructions on ball band.
Place bottle in cover and pull to fit.
Leave to dry.
Cut heart shapes from pink fabric,
arrange on cover and sew in place.

Templates for hearts

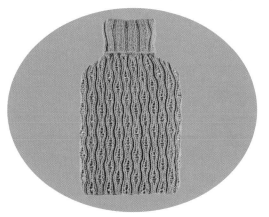

This classy cover is made using a ladder stitch pattern that is deceptively simple. The front is given extra sparkle with knitted-in beads.

Beaded Beauty

Materials
- Rowan Classic Silk Wool DK (91yds/100m per 50g ball)
- 3 x 50g balls shade 305 Clay
- A pair of 4mm (UK8:US6) needles
- A pair of 3.25mm (UK10:US3) needles
- Approx 84 beads (allow a few spares)

Measurements
7½in (19cm) wide (unstretched) x 14½in (37cm) long including top ribbing.

Tension
28 sts x 26 rows to 4in (10cm) over patt using 4mm needles (unstretched)

Special techniques
- Bead 1 = place bead by bringing yarn to front of work; slip bead up to next st, slip next st p-wise to right needle, then take yarn to back of work, leaving bead in front of the slipped st on RS of work.

Front

Thread 72 beads on first ball of yarn.
Using 4mm needles cast on 42 sts.
Row 1 (RS): K all sts.
Row 2: P, inc 10 sts evenly across row
(52 sts).

Pattern

Row 1 (RS): K1, *p2, k1, yon, k1, p2, k2;
rep from *to last 3 sts, p2, k1.
Rows 2, 4 and 6: P1, *k2, p2, k2, p3;
rep from * to last 3 sts, k2, p1.
Row 3 (beads): K1, *p2, k1, bead 1, k1,
p2, k2, rep from * to last 3 sts, p2, k1.
Row 5: K1, *p2, k3, p2, k2; rep from
* to last 3sts, p2, k1.
Row 7: K1, *p2, k1, drop next st and
allow to unravel down to yon six rows
below, k1, p2, k1, yon, k1, rep from * to
last 3 sts, p2, k1.

Tip

*To thread yarn with beads, use a
sewing needle that will pass easily
through the holes in the beads. Fold a
short length of fine thread in half. Pass
both ends through the needle, and
loop yarn through it. Slide beads down
thread and on to yarn.*

Row 8: P1, *k2, p3, k2, p2; rep from * to
last 3 sts, p2, k1.
Row 9 (beads): K1, *p2, k2, p2, k1, bead
1, k1; rep from * to last 3 sts, p2, k1.
Row 10: As row 8.
Row 11: K1, *p2, k2, p2, k3; rep from
* to last 3 sts, p2, k1
Row 12: As row 8.
Row 13: K1, *p2, k1, yon, k1, p2, k1, drop
next st and allow to unravel to yon 6
rows below, k1, rep from * to last 3 sts,
p2, k1.
Cont in patt, rep rows 2-13 throughout,
until cover measures 10½in (26.5cm)
ending with row 6.
Keeping patt correct, cast off 3 sts at beg
of next 6 rows.
Dec 1 st at each end of next 2 rows.
Leave rem 36 sts (incl sts made on row
13) on a spare length on yarn.

Back

Work as for front foll patt but omitting
beads and working these rows thus:
Row 3: K1, *p2, k3, p2, k2; rep from
* to last 3 sts, p2, k1.
Row 9: K1, *p2, k2, p2, k3, rep from * to
last 3 sts, p2, k1.
Cont in patt until back measures 10½in
(26.5cm).
Work top shaping as for front but leave
sts on needle with RS facing for next row.
Thread 12 beads on to a new ball
of yarn.
Change to 3.25mm needles.
K across the 36 sts, dec 6 sts evenly
across row, then transfer sts from spare
yarn to left needle and k across, dec 6 sts
evenly across row, turn.
With RS of collar facing, work the
following:
Row 1: *k3, p2, rep from * to end.
Row 2: *k2, p3, rep from * to end.
Rep these 2 rows until rib measures 6in
(15cm) ending with row 2.
Bead row: *k1, bead 1, k1, p2, rep from
* to end.
Beg with row 2 of rib work 2 rows.
Cast off in rib.

Making up

Join both side seams.
Fold over neck rib.
Slide bottle into cover and join bottom
seam.

This ultra-feminine cover in softest pashmina yarn is inspired by vintage house gowns. The impressive pattern is produced simply by sewing stitches together.

Fabulous Frills

Materials
- Lana Grossa Pashmina (125m per 50g ball)
- 3 x 50g balls shade 05 pink
- A 4.50mm (UK7:US7) circular needle 40cm in length
- 2 x 3mm (UK11:US2–3) or 3.25mm (UK10:US3) double-pointed needles
- Tapestry needle

Measurements
9in (24cm) wide x 14in (37cm) long

Tension
24 sts x 28 rows to 4in (10cm) over stocking stitch using 4.50mm needles

Special techniques
- Making an I-cord (see drawstring, overleaf)

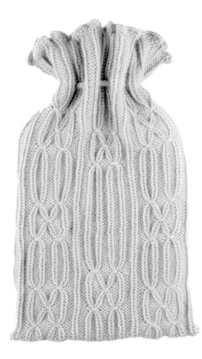

Method

Using 4.50mm circular needle cast on 128 sts and work in rounds.

Round 1: Place marker, p 63, place marker, p to next marker (1 round completed).

Round 2: **p1, k1, * p3, k1, rep from * to st before first marker, p next st, p2, k1, (p3, k1) 15 times, p2.
Rep last round until work measures 4in (10cm).

Divide for centre panel

Next round: P1, k1, (p3, k1) 4 times, p2, k23, p2, k1, (p3, k1) to last 2 sts, p2.
Rep last round until work measures 8in (20cm).
Rep round 2 ** until work measures 12in (30cm).

Next round (eyelets): P1, k1, *p2tog, yo, p1, k1, p3, k1, rep from * to last rep, omitting p3, k1, ending with p2.
Cont in patt as set by round 2 ** for a further 2¼in (6cm).

Next round (frill): Knit into front and back of each st to end (260 sts).

Next round: *knit into front and back of next st, k1, rep from * to end of row (390 sts).
Cast off loosely.

Drawstring

Using 2 double-pointed needles cast on 4 sts and k across but do not turn.
Push sts to other end of needle and pull yarn tight across back.
K across sts again.
Rep until work measures approx 24in (61cm).
Cast off.

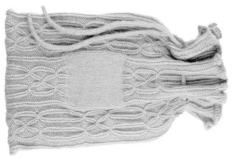

Tip

The central panel has been left plain so it can be decorated with an embroidered initial or motif as preferred. It also looks attractive with toning buttons attached, so just use your imagination!

Making up

Using the markers as a guide, fold the cover so that the plain stocking stitch square is centre front.
Thread a tapestry needle with yarn and work over the rib, joining the knit stitches as shown to form smocking (see photograph)
Join lower edge seams.
Thread drawstring in and out of eyelets, starting and ending at side.
Pull together and tie in a bow.

Men suffer from cold toes too, and this no-frills cover worked
in soft, chunky black yarn is ideal for the man
or the tomboy in your life.

Rugged Cable

Materials

- Nazca Baby Alpaca Chunky (100m per 100g hank)
- 2 x 100g balls black
- A pair of 4mm (UK8:US6) needles
- A pair of pair 4.50mm (UK7:US7) needles
- Cable needle

Measurements

9in (23 cm) wide x 15in total length.

Tension

16 sts x 28 rows to 4in (10cm) over moss stitch using
4.50mm needles

Special techniques

- C6B = place next 6 sts on a cable needle and hold at
  back of work, k next 6 sts, k sts from cable needle.
- Moss stitch

Lower back and front

Using 4.50mm needles cast on 36 sts.
Change to 4mm needles and work in rib.

Rib row 1 (RS): P1, * k2, p2, rep from
* to last 3 sts, k2, p1.

Rib row 2: K1, * p2, k2, rep from
* to last 3 sts, p2, k1.

Rep last 2 rows twice more.**

Change to 4.50mm needles and
work in moss st until work measures
8in (12cm).

Place a marker at each end of last
row to indicate where to fold cover
for front.

Row 1 (RS): Moss st 13 sts, place
marker to delineate cable panel, p2,
k6, p2, place marker, moss st 13.

Row 2: Moss st 13 sts, k2, p6, k2,
moss st 13.

Rep last 2 rows once more.

Row 5: Moss st 13 sts, p2, C6B, p2,
moss st 13.

These rows set the patt.

Work row 2 once, rows 1 and 2 three
times, then work Row 5.

Rep last 8 rows until work measures 10in
(25cm) from markers ending with RS
facing for next row.

Top shaping

Keeping moss st and cable patt correct,
cast off 4 sts at beg of next 2 rows.
Cast off 3 sts at beg of next 2 rows.
Dec1 at each end of foll alt row.
Leave remaining 20 sts on a length
of yarn.

Top back

Using 4.50mm needles cast on 36 sts.
Change to 4.00mm needles and work
in rib.

Rib row 1 (RS): P1, * k2, p2, rep from
* to last 3 sts, k2, p1.

Rib row 2: K1, * p2, k2, rep from * to last 3
sts, p2, k1.

Rep last 2 rows twice more.

Change to 4.50mm needles and work in
moss st until work measures 4½in (11.5cm),
ending with RS facing for next row.

Now work the 6 rows of top shaping as for front but working in moss st only.
Next row (RS): *k2, p2, rep from * to end (20 sts) but do not turn.
With RS facing place sts left on spare yarn on left needle and work row 1 again across these sts, so that you end with 40 sts on right needle, turn.
Change to 4mm needles.
Working in rows, rep row 1 until rib collar measures 7¼ in (18cm).
Cast off loosely in rib.

Making up

Fold cover at markers for lower back.
Join lower front and lower back seams.
Join top front and back seams, overlapping top over lower back seam to form a flap.
Join collar seams and fold rib collar over to form a polo neck.
Make a button loop large enough to slip easily over button at centre edge of top flap.
Attach button to correspond with loop.

Soft and sophisticated, this cover features a subtle cable pattern. Buttons with a natural look complement the luxurious nutmeg alpaca yarn.

Classic Cable

Materials

- Artesano Inca Mist baby alpaca 100% (131yds/120m per 50g ball)
- 2 × 50g balls 0107 Nutmeg
- A pair of 3.25mm (UK10:US3) needles
- A pair of 4mm (UK8:US6) needles
- A cable needle
- 3 × 1in (5cm) buttons

Measurements

10in (25cm) wide × 14¾in (37.5cm) long to top

Tension

25 sts × 32 rows to 4in (10cm) over stocking stitch using 4mm needles

Special techniques

- C8B = slip next 4 sts on to a cable needle and hold at back, k4 from L needle, then k4 from cable needle.
- C8F = slip next 4 sts on to a cable needle and hold at front, k4 from L needle, then k4 from cable needle.

Note: this cover is made in three parts, which are sewn together to form one piece.

Side panel 1

Using 4 mm needles, cast on 12 sts.

Row 1 (RS): K to end.

Row 2: P to last 3 sts, k3.

Rep last 2 rows until work measures 3in (7.5cm).

Place marker at each end of row to indicate where lower edge folds over.

Cont in patt as set until work measures 10½in (27cm) from marker ending with WS facing for next row.

Next row (top shaping): Dec1, work to end.

Work 1 row.

Next row: Cast off 4, work to end.

Next row: Work to 2 sts from end of row, dec 1 st.

Next row: Dec1, work to end.

Cast off rem 5 sts.

Side panel 2

Work as for panel 1, reversing top shaping.

Centre panel

Using 4mm needles, cast on 28 sts and foll 8-row cable patt.

Cable patt

Row 1: P8, k12, p8.

Row 2: K8, p12, k8.

Row 3: P8, k4, C8B, p8.

Row 4: K8, p12, k8.

Rows 5 and 6: As rows 1 and 2

Row 7: P8, C8F, k4, p8

Row 8: K8, p12, k8

When work measures 3in (7.5cm), place markers at each end of row.

Cont in patt, placing second set of markers at each end of row when work measures 13¾in (35cm).

Top neck shaping

Next 4 rows: Dec 1 st each end of row.

Work straight for 4 rows

Next 4 rows: Inc 1 st each end of row.

Work straight until top shaping measures 6½in (16.5cm) from last marker.

Next 4 rows: Dec 1 st each end of row.

Work straight for 4 rows.

Next 4 rows: Inc 1 st each end **.

Place marker for start of main body of cover.

Work straight, foll patt as set, until work measures 28¼in (72cm).

Cast off.

Side edgings for centre panel

Pick up and knit 84 sts evenly along one side edge of centre panel to second marker.

Work 4 rows g-st (every row knit).

Cast off k-wise.

Rep on other side of panel, beg at second marker and working down.

Side edgings for upper back

With RS of centre panel facing and beg at neck marker** pick up and knit 36 sts.

Next row: K to end.

Rep last row 3 times more.

Cast off k-wise.

Rep on other side, beg at cast off edge up to next marker.

Top back edging

Using 3.25mm needles and with RS of work facing pick up and knit 52 sts along lower edge of top back. Work 4 rows g-st

Next row (buttonhole): K8, (cast off 2, k14) x 2, cast off 2, k7.

Next row: Work in g-st, casting on 2 sts over the sts cast off on previous row.

Cont in g-st until work measures the same as bottom back rib.

Cast off k-wise.

Making up

Join all sides, overlapping g-st rib to form button band.

Attach buttons to correspond to buttonholes.

Joining panels

Dry press side panels but not centre panel. Lay out pieces, matching markers, and join neatly.

Lower back edging

Using 3.25 needles and with RS facing pick up and knit 52 sts along lower edge of cover.

Work in g-st for ¾in (2cm) ending with WS facing.

Cast off k-wise.

This fine-knit retro cover is brought up to date by soft salmon yarn.
Mother-of-pearl buttons sparkle like water on leaping fish.

Vintage Buttons

Materials

- Lane Borgosesia Bollicina 4-ply (155yds per 25g ball)
- 3 x 25g balls shade N67
- A pair of 2.75mm (UK12:US2) needles
- A pair of 2.25mm (UK13–14:US0-1) needles
- 16 x ½in (1.3cm) mother-of-pearl buttons

Measurements

9in (23cm) wide x 14½in (37cm) long including top ribbing

Tension

32 sts x 40 rows to 4in (10cm) over stocking stitch using 2.75mm needles

Special techniques

- Reverse stocking stitch = work as stocking stitch but use the ridged side as the right side

Left front

Using 2.75mm needles and main yarn, cast on 40 sts.

Next row (RS): P to end.

Next row: Cast on 5, k to end.

Next row: Cast on 5, p to end.

Next 2 rows: Cast on 4, work to end.

Still working in reverse st st, inc 1 st at each end of next 3 rows (68 sts).

Next row (RS): P to end

Next row: K to end.

Next row: P34, turn and leave rem 34 sts on spare length of yarn.

Work a further 9 rows reverse st st on first 34 sts.

Next row: *p to end, cast on 8.

Work 5 rows.

Buttonhole row: P to last 5 sts, yrn, p2tog, p3.

Work 4 rows.

Next row: Cast off 8, k to end.

Work 8 rows.

Repeat from * 3 times more.

Next row: P to end, cast on 8.

Work 1 row.

Neck shaping

Next row (RS): Dec1 at beg of row, work to end.

Next row: Work to last 2 sts, K2tog.

Next row (RS): Dec1 at beg of row, work to end.

Work 1 row.

Next row: Cast off 2, p to last 5 sts, yrn, p2tog, p3.

Work 1 row.

Next row (RS): Cast off 4, work to end of row.

Work 1 row

Next row (RS): Cast off 5, work to end of row.

Work 1 row.

Leave sts on spare length of yarn.

Right front

Return to 34 sts left on spare length of yarn and place on left needle.

Next row (RS): P to end.

Next row: **k to end, cast on 8.

Work 4 rows.

Next row (buttonhole): P3, p2tog, yrn, p to end.

Work 5 rows.

Next row: Cast off 8, p to end.

Work 8 rows. **

Rep from ** to ** 4 times more, but work only 1 row at end of last repeat.

Neck shaping

Next row: Work to last 2 sts, dec.

Next row: Dec1, work to end.

Next row: Work to last 2 sts, dec.

Next row: Cast off 2, work to end.

Work 1 row.

Next row: Cast off 4, work to end.

Work 1 row.

Next row: Cast off 5, work to end.

Work 1 row.

Leave sts on spare length of yarn.

Back

Using 2.75mm needles, cast on 40 sts.

Next row: P to end.

Next 2 rows: Cast on 5, work to end.

Next 2 rows: Cast on 4, work to end.

Next 2 rows: Cast on 2, work to end.

Next 3 rows: Inc 1 st at each end row.

Next row: P to end.

Cont in rev st st for a further 93 rows.

Neck rib

Change to 2.25mm needles. With WS of cover facing and RS of collar work thus:

Row 1: K2, *p3, k2; rep from * to end.

Row 2: *p2, k3; rep from * to last 2 sts, p2.

Rep last 2 rows until rib measures 6½in (16.5cm).

Cast off in rib.

Tie

Using 2.25mm needles cast on 4 sts, leaving a short length of yarn to thread on a needle and weave in and out of eyelets.

Work in g-st (every row k) until tie measures 17¼in (44cm).

Cast off k-wise.

Making up

Overlap front flaps (see photograph) and attach buttons to correspond to buttonholes (5 buttons each side of front).

Join side and bottom seams.

Join collar, reversing seam for turn-over.

Thread tie through eyelets beginning and ending at side of cover.

Attach 3 buttons to each end of tie.

Place bottle in front of cover; fasten buttons, tie and knot.

Neck shaping

Next row (RS): P to end.

Next 3 rows: Dec1, work to end.

Next 2 rows: Cast off 2, work to end.

Next 2 rows: Cast off 4, work to end.

Next 2 rows: Cast off 5, work to end.

Next row: P across, then transfer all but 8 sts sts placed on spare yarn after working left front to needle and purl across (8 sts still on yarn). Transfer sts placed on spare yarn after working right front to needle. Using 1 st from spare yarn and 1 st from left needle, p2tog (8 times). Purl across rem sts (80 sts).

Next row (10 eyelets): K7, *k2tog, yrn, k5; rep from * 8 times, k2tog, yrn, k8.

Next row: Purl, inc 2 sts evenly across the row.

This dainty cover with a vintage feel is made from smooth cotton.
The delicate lace pattern is easier than it looks.

Dragon Lace

Materials

- Isager Mercerised Cotton (252 yds/230m per 100g ball)
- 1 x 100g ball green shade 40
- Oddment of red yarn
- A pair of 3.25mm (UK10:US3) needles
- A pair of 3mm (UK11:US2–3) needles
- Crochet hook to make drawstring
- 3 x medium-sized toning buttons

Measurements

8½in (23cm) wide by 10¾in (27.5cm) long excluding rib

Tension

28 sts x 36 rows to 4in (10cm) over stocking stitch using 3.25mm needles

Special techniques

- Ssk = slip 1 st k-wise, slip 1 st p-wise, insert left needle into front loops of slipped sts and k2 tog through the back loops
- M1 = make 1 stitch

Front

Using 3.25mm needles cast on 64 sts.

Row 1 (RS): K all sts.

Row 2: P all sts.

Now foll patt bleow until work measures 10¼in (26cm) ending with a p row.

Lace pattern

Row 1: K2, *k1, m1, ssk, k5, k2tog, k4, m1, k2, m1, k4, ssk, k5, k2tog, m1, k1; rep from * once more, k2.

Row 2 and every alt row: P to end.

Row 3: K2, * k1, m1, k2, ssk, k2, k2tog, k5, m1, k2, m1, k5, ssk, k2, k2tog, k2, m1, k1; rep from * once, k2.

Row 5: K2, * k1, m1, k3, ssk, k2tog, k6, m1, k2, m1, k6, ssk, k2tog, k3, m1, k1; rep from * once, k2.

Row 7: K2, * k1, m1, k4, ssk, k5, k2tog, m1, k2, m1, ssk, m5, k2tog, k4, m1, k1; rep from * once, k2.

Row 9: K2, * k1, m1, k5, ssk, k2, k2tog, k2, m1, k2, m1, k2, ssk, k2, k2tog, k5, m1, k1; rep from * once, k2.

Row 11: K2, *k1, m1, k6, ssk, k2tog, k3, m1, k2, m1, k3, ssk, k2tog, k6, m1, k1; rep from * once, k2.

Row 12: P to end.

Neck shaping

Cast off 7 sts at beg of next 2 rows.

Cast off 8 sts at beg of next 2 rows (34 sts).

Next row (eyelets): K6, *yrn, k2tog, k5, rep from * 3 times.

Next row: P all sts.

Leave sts on spare length of yarn.

Lower back

Using 3.25mm needles, cast on 60 sts.

Beg with a k row, work in st st until work measures 7¼in (18cm), ending with RS facing for next row.

Change to 3mm needles.

Next row (button band): K1, p2, * k2, p2; rep from * to last st, k1.

Next row: P1, *k2, p2; rep from * to last 3 sts, k2, p1.

Rep these 2 rows 3 times more.

Cast off in rib.

Upper back

Using 3mm needles, cast on 60 sts.
Work 3 rows as for button band on
lower back.

Next row (buttonholes): *rib 13, cast
off 3 sts; rep from * 3 times, rib 12.

Next row: work in rib as set, casting on
3 sts over the 3 sts cast off on
previous row.

Work 3 further rows rib, ending with RS
facing for next row.

Change to 3.25mm needles.

Work in st st, beg with a k row, until
work measures 3in (7.5cm) from cast-on
edge ending with RS facing for next row

Neck shaping

Cast off 7 sts at beg of next 2 rows
(46 sts).

Cast off 8 sts at beg of next row (38 sts).

Next row: Cast off 8 sts, inc 4 sts evenly
across rem 30 sts (34 sts).

Next row (eyelets): K6, *yrn, k2tog, k5,
rep from * 3 times.

Next row: P all sts.

Change to 3mm needles.

Rib collar

Row 1: *k2, p2; rep from * across back;
transfer sts left on spare yarn to left
needle and cont in rib as set to end of
row (68 sts).

Rep this row until rib measures 6¾in
(17cm) ending with RS of collar facing.
Cast off in rib.

Making up

Press lightly, using a damp cloth.
Join lower front and back seam, upper
front and back seam, overlapping
buttonhole band over button band.
Join rib collar, reversing seam halfway to
allow collar to be folded.

Drawstring

Using the oddment of red yarn double,
crochet a chain 16in (41cm) long.
Weave drawstring through eyelets, beg
and ending at one side of cover.

Diamonds (make 2)

Using red yarn and 3mm needles, cast
on 2 sts and work in g-st (every row
knit).

Work 1 row.

Next row: Inc1, work to end.

Rep last row until there are 9 sts on
needle.

Work 1 row.

Next row: Dec 1, work to end.

Rep this row until 2 sts rem.

Next row: Skpo.

Fasten off and attach to end of chain.

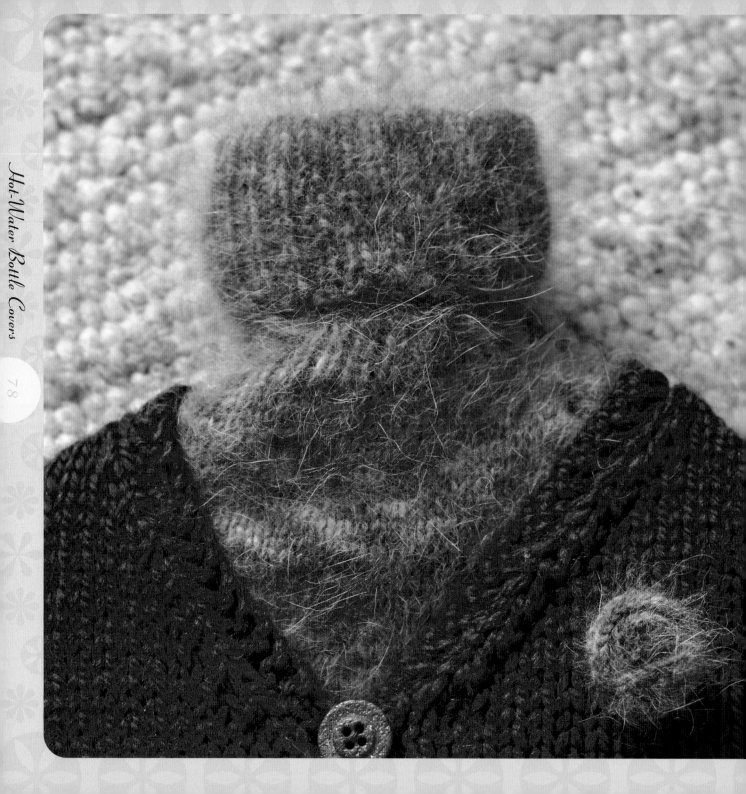

Dress your bottle in a fluffy polo topped by a chunky waistcoat.
It was inspired by the mismatched chunky buttons
that add a funky touch.

Wacky Waistcoat

Materials
- Anny Blatt Angora Super (116yds/106m per 50g ball)
- 2 x 50g balls shade 454 Pourpre (A)
- Bouton d'Or Laika (54yds per 50g ball)
- 3 x 50g balls shade 290 Ketchup (B)
- A pair of 3.25mm (UK10:US3) needles
- A pair of 4mm (UK8:US6) needles
- A pair of 5.50mm (UK5:US9) needles
- A pair of 6mm (UK4:US10) needles
- 3 assorted toning buttons

Measurements
8¾in (22cm) wide × 14½ (37cm) long

Tension
23 sts × 30 rows to 4in (10cm) over stocking stitch using 4mm needles and A
15 sts × 20 rows to 4in (10cm) over stocking stitch using 6mm needles and B

Special techniques
- The cover is worked in two pieces

Polo top (front)

Using 3.25mm needles and A, cast on 48 sts.

Next row (RS): *k1, p1; rep from * to end.

Rep this row 3 more times.

Change to 4mm needles and work in st st, beg with a k row, until top measures 5in (12.5cm) from cast-on edge, ending with RS facing for next row.

Top shaping

Next 3 rows: Dec 1 st at each end.
Work 1 row.

Cast off 3 sts at beg of next 2 rows.
Cast off 4 sts at beg of next 2 rows (28 sts).
Leave rem sts on a spare length of yarn.

Polo top (back)

Work exactly as front but leave sts on needle.

Change to 3.25mm needles.

Next row (RS): *k1, p1; rep from * across row.

Transfer sts from spare yarn to left needle and work in k1, p1 rib across these sts.

Next row: K1, p1 to end.
Rep this row until rib measures 6¼in (16cm).
Cast off in rib.

Cardigan
Pocket linings (make 2)

Using 6mm needles and B, cast on 8 sts.
Work 8 rows st st.
Leave sts on a spare length of yarn.

Back

Using 6mm needles and B, cast on 20 sts and work in st st throughout.

Next row (RS): K all sts.
Inc 1 st at each end of next row.
Cast on 3 sts at beg of next 4 rows.
Next row: K all sts.
Next row: P all sts.
Rep last 2 rows until 50 rows in total have been worked from cast-on edge, ending with RS facing for next row.

Top back shaping

Next 3 rows: Dec 1 st at each end of the row.
Cast off 3 sts at beg of next 2 rows.
Cast off rem 22 sts.

Right front

Using 6mm needles and B, cast on 11 sts.
Next row (RS): K all sts
Next row: Inc1, p to last 2 sts, k2.
Next row: K all sts.
Next row: Cast on 3 sts at beg of row, p to last 2 sts, k2.
Rep last 2 rows once more (18 sts).

Cont in st st keeping the 2 st g-st edging as set until 14 rows have been worked from cast-on edge, ending with RS facing for next row.

Next row (place pocket, RS): K5, place next 8 sts on a spare length of yarn for pocket top, transfer one set of pocket lining sts to needle and k across, k5, turn. Cont as set until 32 rows in total have been worked, ending with RS facing for next row.

Next row (buttonhole): K1, yrn, k2tog, k to end.

Next row: P to last 2 sts, k2.

Next row: K all sts.

Next row: P to last 2 sts, place these 2 sts on a safety pin for front edging.

Next row: K all sts.

Next row: P to last 2 sts, p2tog.

Next row: K all sts.

Rep last 2 rows until 10 sts rem.

Dec1 at end of next 2 rows.

Dec1 at each end of next row.

Dec1 at end of next row.

Next row: Cast off 3 sts at beg of next row, work to last 2 sts, dec1.

Next row: K all sts.

Cast off.

Left front

Using 6mm needles and B, cast on 11 sts.

Next row: K all sts.

Next row: K2, p to last st, inc1.

Next row: Cast on 3 sts at beg, k to end.

Next row: K2, p to end of row.

Next row: Cast on 3 sts, k to end.

Cont in st st keeping the 2-st g-st edging as set until 14 rows have been worked from cast-on edge.

Next row (place pocket): Work as for right front.

Cont as set until 36 rows in total have been worked.

Next row: K to last 2 sts, place these 2 sts on a safety pin for front edging.

Next row: Dec1, p to end.

Next row: K to end.

Rep last 2 rows until 10 sts rem.

Next 2 rows: Dec1, work to end.

Next row: Dec1, work to end.

Next 2 rows: Dec1, work to end.

Cast off 3 sts at beg of next row.

Next row: P to end.

Cast off.

Pocket tops

Using 5.50mm needles and B, pick up and k one set of 8 sts left on spare yarn, turn.

Work 2 more rows g-st.

Cast off k-wise.

Rep for other pocket top.

Front edgings

Using 5.50mm needles and beg at right front, transfer the 2 sts left on safety pin to needles and work in g-st, beg with a k row, until edging fits up right front across to centre back.

Rose

Using 3.25mm needles and A, cast on 10 sts.

Row 1 (RS): K all sts.

Row 2: P all sts.

Row 3: K into the front and back of each st (20 sts).

Row 4: P all sts.

Row 5: Rep row 3.

Rows 6 and 7: K all sts.

Cast off k-wise.

Making up

Sew front edgings in place.

Rep for left front, sewing cast-off edges tog at back.

Attach button to correspond to buttonhole.

Sew down pocket edges using slip st.

Join side and bottom seams overlapping the g-st edge at base of cover.

Attach rem buttons, sewing through both left and right front g-st edge.

Shape rose by folding twice anticlockwise to form a tight circle, secure in place and attach to top left front (see photograph).

Join side seams of polo top and polo neck, reversing seam to allow it to be folded.

Place polo top over bottle, then place bottle in the cardigan with the shoulders over the top bottle shaping, and fasten button to hold in place.

This clever design makes innovative use of a beautiful silk mix
random yarn – watch the shades change before your eyes
as the cover is worked.

Ingenious Entrelac

Materials

- Noro Silk Garden (109yds per 50g ball)
- 3 x 50g balls shade 11
- A pair of 4mm (UK8:US6) needles
- A pair of 3.75mm (UK9:US5) needles

Measurements

Length 14½in (37cm) including top rib and 18in (46cm)
wide before cover is folded

Tension

24 sts x 32 rows to 10cm over st st using 4mm needles

Special techniques

- Inc = increase by working into front and back of stitch
- Skpo = slip one stitch, knit one stitch, pass slipped
  stitch over
- Pick up sts from the 'knot' at the end of rows for a
  neater finish avoiding gaps

Note: Cover is worked to fit round bottle widthwise

Cover (in one piece)

Using 4mm needles cast on 40 sts loosely. K one row.

Base triangles

Row 1: *p2 (ws), turn
Row 2: K2, turn.
Row 3: P3, turn.
Row 4: K3, turn.
Row 5: P4, turn.
Row 6: K4, turn.

Cont in this way, working 1 st more on every WS row until the row K7, turn has been worked.

Next row: P8 but do not turn. Move along to next 2 sts on needle and rep from * until 5 triangles have been made.

First edge triangle

Row 1: K2, turn.
Row 2: P2, turn.
Row 3: Inc in first st, skpo, turn.
Row 4: P3, turn.
Row 5: Inc in first st, k1, skpo, turn.

Row 6: P4, turn.
Row 7: Inc in first st, k2, skpo, turn.
Row 8: P5, turn.
Row 9: Inc in first st, k3, skpo, turn.
Row 10: P6, turn.
Row 11: Inc in first st, k4, skpo, turn.
Row 12: P7, turn.
Row 13: Inc in first st, k5, skpo but do not turn.

First set of rectangles

Row 1: *pick up and k8 evenly along edge of next triangle, turn.
Row 2: P8, turn.
Row 3: K7, skpo, turn.

Rep last 2 rows 8 times but do not turn on last row (1 rectangle complete).
Rep from * to edge of last triangle, pick up and k8 evenly along triangle, turn.
Next row: P2tog, p6, turn.
Next row: K7, turn.
Next row: P2tog, p5, turn.
Next row: K6, turn.
Cont in this way until 'P2 tog, p1, turn' has been worked.
Next row: K2, turn.
Next row: P2tog (edge triangle complete leaving 1 st on right needle).

Second set of rectangles

Rectangle 1: Cont from st on right needle, pick up (p-wise) and p7 evenly along edge of triangle just worked, (turn, k8, turn and p7, p2tog) 8 times.

Rectangle 2: *pick up and p8 evenly along side of next rectangle, (turn and k8, turn and p7, p2 tog) 8 times.
Rep from * to end.

Third set of rectangles

As first row but pick up sts along side edge of rectangles.

Work as set until cover measures approx 18in (46cm), ending with a completed third set of rectangles.

Triangle 1: *cont from st on R needle, pick up (p-wise) and p7 evenly along edge of triangle just worked, turn, k8, turn, p2tog, p5, p2tog, turn, k7, turn, p2tog, p4, p2tog, turn, k6, turn, p2 tog, p3, p2tog.

Cont as set working 1 st less between decs on every WS row until the row 'k3', has been worked, turn.

Next row: (p2tog) twice, turn.

Next row: K2, turn.

Next row: P1, p2tog, p1, turn k3, turn, p3tog.

Rep from * to end but pick up sts along side of rectangle instead of triangle.
Fasten off rem st.

Making up

Pin out and damp press lightly.
Fold cover so that both ends meet at centre back and sew top seams allowing 4½in (11.5cm) opening to work collar. Do not join back seams.

Rib collar

Using 3.75mm needles and beg at left back seam with RS facing, pick up and k13 to front seam, k22 across front to right front seam, k13 to right back edge (48 sts).

Row 1: *k2, p2, rep from * to end.
Rep this row until rib measures 7½in (19cm).
Cast off in rib.

Finishing

Join back and collar seams, reversing neck seam half-way to allow collar to be folded over to RS.
Slide in bottle and join bottom seam.

Inspired by the shape of buildings against the Big Apple's skyline, this cover uses tweed-effect yarn in subtle shades that complement each other perfectly.

New York

Materials

- Rowan Summer Tweed (108m per 50g ball)
- 1 x 50g ball burnt orange shade 542 Mango (A)
- 1x 50g ball yellow shade 538 Butter Ball (B)
- 1 x 50g ball green shade 513 Dew (C)
- 1 x 50g ball blue shade 511 Cape (D)
- A pair of 4.50mm (UK7:US7) needles
- A pair of 5mm (UK6:US8) needles
- 2 x medium buttons

Measurements

8½in (21.5cm) wide x 14½in (37cm) total length

Tension

16 sts x 23 rows to 4in (10cm) over st st using 5mm needles

Special techniques

- Cover is worked throughout using the Intarsia method and st st. The colour blocks will for both upper and lower back be opposite to the front.

Note: when working the lower back, turn the chart upside-down to make it easier to follow.

Lower back and front (worked as one piece)

Using 4.50mm needles and D, cast on 34 sts.

Row 1: *k1, p1, rep from * to end.
Rep this row 7 times more.
Change to 5mm needles and begin to work in st st, foll upside-down chart and joining in yarn as necessary.

Next row: With RS facing and beg with row 42 of chart, k11D, k9C, k3A, k11B.
Cont until row 1 of chart has been completed.
Place marker each end of last row to indicate lower edge.

Front

Turn chart the right way up and foll from row 1 to row 82 (inclusive).
Place marker each end of last row to indicate where to fold for top.

Upper back

Turn chart upside-down and foll from and including row 82 until row 51 has been completed, still working in st st.
Change to 4.50mm needles.

Buttonhole band

Row 1: Using D only, *k1, p1, rep from * to end.
Rep last row 3 times more.
Next row: Rib 10, cast off 2, rib 9, cast off 2, rib to end.
Next row: Work in rib as set casting on 2 sts over cast-off sts of previous row.
Work 2 more rows rib.
Cast off in rib.

Making up

Press, following directions on ball band.
Fold cover from both sets of markers, matching up top shaping, and pin in place.
Overlap the ribbing so the buttonhole band is uppermost. Join all seams.
Attach buttons to correspond to buttonholes.

New York Chart
(34 sts, 82 rows)

C
B
A
D

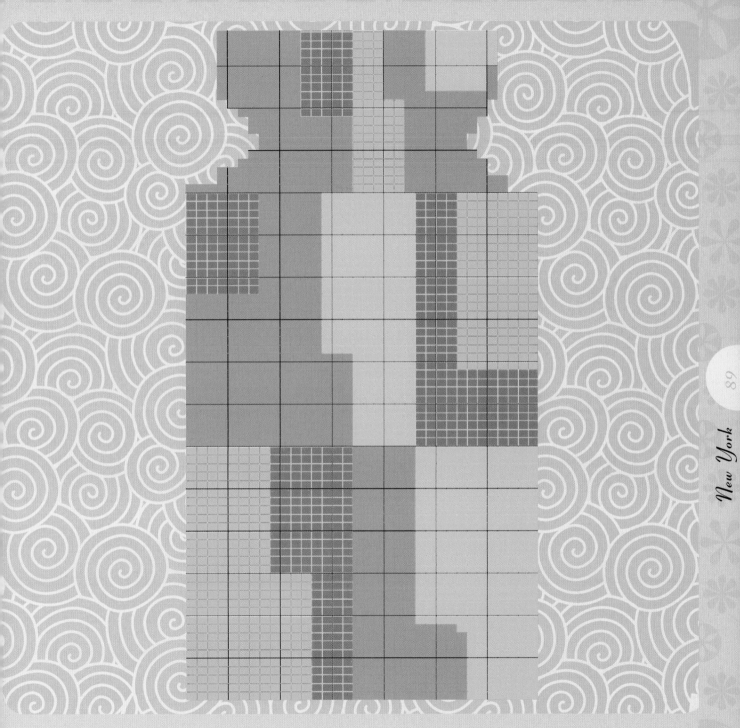

Show someone that you care with this gorgeous cover in supersoft mohair yarn, decorated with tiny hearts and cables.

Purple Heart

Materials

- Rowan Kid Classic (140m per 50g ball)
- 2 x 50g balls shade 835 Royal (M)
- 1 x 50g ball shade 841 Lavender Ice (C)
- A pair of 5mm (UK6:US8) needles
- 2 x 3.75mm (UK9:US5) double-pointed needles
- Cable needle

Measurements

8½in (21.5cm) wide × 14½in (37cm) total length

Tension

16 sts and 22 rows to 4in (10cm)
over sr st using 5mm needles

Special techniques

- C4B = slip 2 sts on to cable needle and hold at back of work, knit next 2 sts, then k sts from cable needle
- C4F = slip 2 sts on to cable needle and hold at front of work, knit next 2 sts, then k sts from cable needle.

Front

Using M, cast on 27 sts.
Working the hearts in C and using the intarsia method, follow chart until row 76 has been worked.
Leave rem 37 sts on a spare length of yarn.

Back

Work as for front but leave sts on needle.
Next row (RS): K across 37 sts on needle, then transfer sts from spare yarn to L needle and k across sts (74 sts).

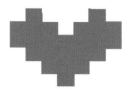

Top rib

Row 1: * p1, k1, rep from * to end.
Rep last row until rib measures 2in (5cm) ending with RS facing for next row.
Next row (eyelets): Rib 3, *k2tog, yrn, rib 4, rep from * 11 times, k2 tog, yrn, rib 3.
Next row: *p1, k1, rep from * to end
Rep last row until rib measures 3¼in (9cm) in total.
Cast off in rib.

Cord

Using 3.75mm double pointed needles and C, cast on 4 sts.
Next row: *k4 but do not turn; push sts to other end of needle, pull yarn tight and k4 again.
Rep from * until cord measures 24–26in (61–66cm).

Making up

Pin out both pieces carefully and press lightly.
Join sides and bottom edge.
Thread cord through the eyelets, beginning and ending at the side of cover; pull cord to tighten ribbing and tie in a bow.

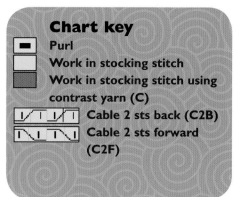

Chart key

- ▬ Purl
- Work in stocking stitch
- Work in stocking stitch using contrast yarn (C)
- Cable 2 sts back (C2B)
- Cable 2 sts forward (C2F)

Purple Heart Chart
(47 stitches, 76 rows)

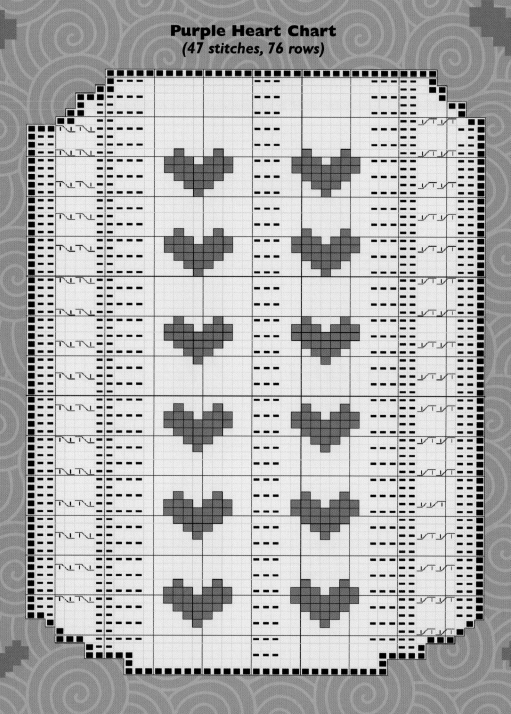

Purple Heart

Seaside sketches inspired this cover in beautiful latte and ocean shades. Big and little hearts are worked in a luxurious mix of cashmere, merino and silk.

Harmonious Hearts

Materials

- Sirdar Sublime cashmere merino silk aran
- 2 x 50g balls shade 0056 Coffee (M)
- 1 x 50g ball shade 0060 Coast (C)
- A pair of 5mm needles
- 2 x 3mm or 3.25mm double-pointed needles

Measurements

9in (23cm) wide x 15in (38cm) long including ribbing

Tension

18 sts x 24 rows to 4in (10cm) over st st using 5mm needles

Special techniques

- Intarsia
- Making an I-cord (see drawstring, page 96)

Front and back (make 2 alike)

Using 5mm needles and M, cast on 27 sts and work in st st.

Row 1 (RS): K all sts.

Cast on 4 sts at the beg of next 2 rows.

Cast on 3 sts at the beg of next 2 rows.

Next row: Inc1 at each end (43 sts). Follow chart, working the hearts in C, until row 71 has been worked.

Next row: Dec1 at each end of row.

Cast off 3 sts at the beg of next 2 rows.

Dec1 at each end of next row (33 sts). Leave sts on a spare length of yarn.

Back

Work as for front but leave sts on needle.

Next row (WS): P across sts on needle, transfer sts from spare length of yarn to needle and p across (66 sts).

Rib collar

Using 5mm needle and M only *k1, p1, rep from * to end.

Rep last row until collar measures 1¼in (3cm) ending with RS facing for the next row.

Next row (eyelets): Rib 4, k2tog,* rib 6, k2tog, yo, rep from* to last 4 sts, rib 4. Cont in rib as set for 5 rows ending with RS facing for next row.

Drawstring

Using 2 double-pointed needles and C, cast on 4 sts.

Next row: K4 but do not turn. Push sts to far end of needle, pull yarn tight and k4 again.

Rep until string measures 24in (61cm).

Making up

Damp press pieces.

Join the 3 sides of cover and side collar seams.

Thread drawstring through eyelets beg and end at the side, pull cord to tighten ribbing and tie in a bow.

Harmonious Hearts Chart
(43 stitches, 71 rows)

Harmonious Hearts

This clever cover has an abstract geometric design reminiscent of old-fashioned quilts. The added top-stitching enhances the patchwork effect.

Pretty Patchwork

Materials

- Lane Borgosesia Otto Aran-weight yarn (135yds/123m per 50g ball)
- 1 x 50g ball shade 689 Antique Lavender (M)
- 1 x 50g ball shade 42000 Ash (C)
- Oddment of shade 26912 Magenta
- A pair of 4.50mm (UK7:US7) needles
- A pair of 3.75mm (UK9:US5)knitting needles
- Blunt-ended tapestry needle
- 4 medium buttons

Measurements

9¼in (23.5cm) wide × 14½in (37cm) long

Tension

20 sts × 28 rows to 4in (10cm) over stocking stitch using 4.50mm needles

Special techniques

Main body of cover is worked using the Intarsia method

Front, collar, upper back and buttonhole (worked in one piece)

Using M and 4.50mm needles cast on 24 sts.

Next row (RS): K all sts.

Follow chart from row 2, working in st st and using the Intarsia method changing and joining in colours where indicated.

At the same time work the following:

Cast on 6 sts at beg of next 2 rows.

Inc 1 st at each end of next 4 rows.

Inc 1 st at each end of foll alt row (46 sts).

Work straight until row 59 has been completed, ending with WS facing for next row.

Dec 1 st at each end of next 4 rows.

Cast off 3 sts at beg of next 2 rows.

Cast off 2 sts at beg of next 2 rows.

Dec 1 st at each end of next 2 rows (24 sts).

Next row (WS): P all sts, using M.

Change to 3.75mm needles.

Next row (collar): Still using M, p1, *k2, p2, rep from * to last 3 sts, k2, p1.

Next row: K1, *p2, k2, rep from * to last 3 sts, p2, k1.

Rep last 2 rows until collar measures 8in (20cm), ending with RS facing for the next row.

Change to 4.50mm needles and M and work 1 row.

Next row: P all sts.

Now work chart downward in st st from row 96 to row 45, and at the same time work the following:

Inc 1 st at each end of next 2 rows.

Cast on 2 sts at beg of next 2 rows.

Cast on 3 sts at beg of next 2 rows.

Inc 1 st at each end of next 4 rows.

Work straight, following chart, until row 45 has been completed.

Change to 3.75mm needles and work in M.

Row 1 of rib: *k2, p2, rep from * to last 2 sts, k2.

Row 2 of rib: *p2, k2, rep from * to last 2 sts, p2.

Work 2 more rows rib.

Next row (buttonhole): Rib 8, *cast off 2, rib 5, rep from *twice more, cast off 2, rib 8.

Next row: Rib 8, *cast on 2, rib 5, rep from * twice more, cast on 2, rib 8.

Work rows 4 more rows of rib.

Cast off in rib.

Lower back

Work as for front until row 33 of chart has been completed (starting at row1).

Change to 3.75mm needles and using C only.

Row 1: *p2, k2, rep from * to last 2 sts, p2.

Row 2: *k2, p2, rep from * to last 2 sts, k2.

Rep last 2 rows 4 times more.

Cast off in rib.

Making up

Using C, embroider front and back of cover as indicated by chart.

Press, following directions on ball band.

Join lower back to front lower back.

Fold over top back, overlapping rib section, and sew in place.

Attach buttons to correspond with buttonholes.

Chart key	
M	**Main colour**
C	**Contrast colour**
O	**French knot**
—	**Top stitching**

Pretty Patchwork Chart
(46 stitches, 96 rows)

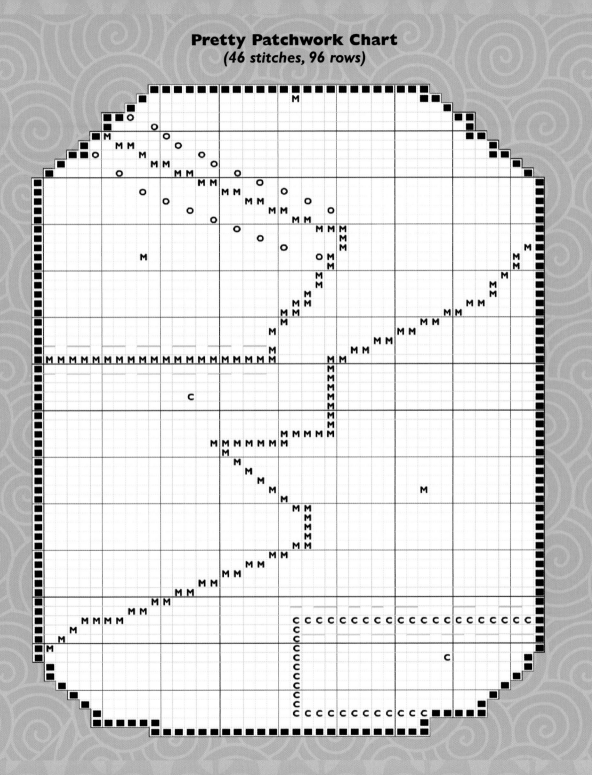

This traditional paisley design is inspired by smoking jackets from the past. Soft teals and aqua bring the pattern right up to the minute.

Perfect Paisley

Materials

- Rowan Felted Tweed (175m per 50g ball)
- 2 × 50g balls shade 153 brown (A)
- Rowan Summer Tweed (108m/118 yds per 50g ball)
- 1 × 50g ball shade 538 yellow (B)
- 1 × 50g ball shade 511 (blue) (C)
- A pair of 4mm (UK8:US6) needles
- A pair of 3.75mm (UK9:US5) needles
- 2 × 3.75mm double-pointed needles

Measurements

8½in (22cm) wide × 14in (35cm) long in total

Tension

22 sts × 30 rows to 4in (10cm) over st st using 4mm needles and Felted Tweed

Special techniques

- The cover is worked using the intarsia method, using separate balls of yarn for each block of colour and joining in colours where indicated.

Front and back (work 2)

Using A and 4mm needles, cast on 48 sts. With RS facing and beg with a knit row follow chart from row 1 to 88 inclusive, working in st st throughout.

Next row (eyelets): K8, * k2tog, yrn, k8, rep from * 3 times more.

Top frill

Work in st st until cover measures 13¾in (35cm) ending with WS facing for the next row.

Change to 3.75mm needles.

Work 4 rows g-st.

Cast off k-wise.

Drawstring

Using the double-pointed needles and A, cast on 4 sts.

Next row: K4 but do not turn; push sts to other end of needle, pull the yarn tight and k4 again.

Rep from * until cord measures 24–26in (61–66cm).

Cast off.

Sew in ends.

Making up

Damp press pieces.

Join side and bottom seams.

Thread cord through eyelets beginning and ending at the side of cover; pull to tighten round neck of bottle and tie in a bow.

Pretty Paisley Chart
(48 stitches, 90 rows)

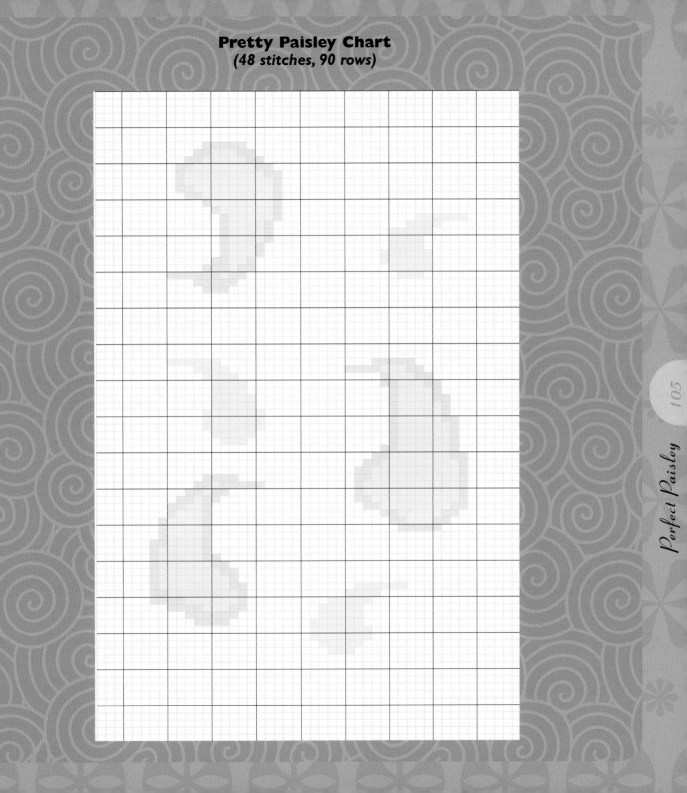

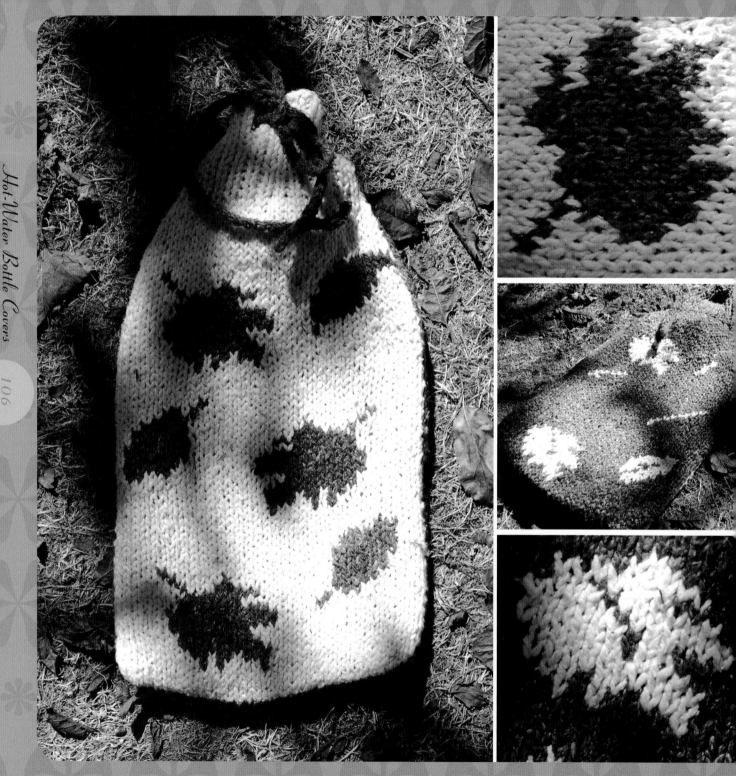

Lovely autumnal shades, a gorgeous tweed-effect yarn and a lively design make the leaves seem almost to be flying off the cover.

Autumn Leaves

Materials

- Rowan Summer Tweed (118yds/108m per 50g skein)
- 1 x 50g skein Cream 524
- 1 x 50g skein Brown 530
- 1 x 50g skein Tan 536
- A pair of 4.50mm (UK7:US7) needles
- A pair of 5mm (UK5:US9) needles
- A 4.50mm (UK7:US7) crochet hook

Measurements

9in (23cm) wide x 15in (38cm) long (including top rib)

Tension

16 sts x 23 rows to 4in (10cm) over stocking stitch using 5mm needles

Special techniques

- Cover is worked in stocking stitch using the Intarsia method.

Front

Using 5mm needles and cream as main colour, cast on 36 sts.

With RS facing and beg with row 1 foll chart, joining in contrast colours where indicated, until row 64 has been completed.

With RS facing and still using cream, cast off 2 sts beg of next 4 rows (28 sts).

Top rib

Change to 4.50mm needles.

Next row: Using cream, *k1, p1, rep from * to end.

Rep last row until rib measures 1½in (4cm) ending with RS facing.

Eyelet row: K1, p1, k1, *yrn, k2tog, rib 5, rep from * to last 4 sts, yrn, k2tog, rib 2.

Cont in rib until work measures 2¾in (7cm) in total.

Cast off in rib.

Back

Using 5mm needles and tan as main colour, cast on 36 sts.

Follow chart as for front, but working the leaves as indicated for back.

Top rib

Using tan, work ribbing as for front.

Eyelet row: Work as for front

Cont as set for front.

Fasten off.

Drawstring

Using 4.50mm crochet hook and two lengths of brown, make a chain 28in (72cm) long.

Fasten off and weave in ends.

Note: the drawstring may be made by finger knitting or plaiting if preferred.

Making up

Damp press pieces, following instructions on ball band.

Join side and bottom seams using mattress stitch.

Thread drawstring through eyelets, beginning and ending at centre front.

Pull to fit neck of bottle and tie in a bow.

Autumn Leaves Chart
(36 stitches, 70 rows)

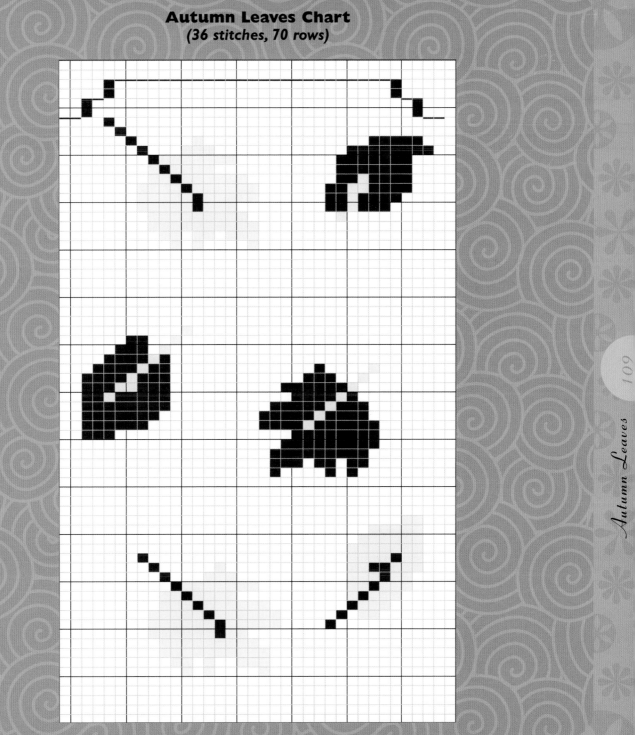

Autumn Leaves

Snuggly soft yarn and lipstick shades in classic Fair Isle stitches make this sumptuous cover the perfect gift for a 'girly' girl.

Feminine Fair Isle

Materials

- Sublime Angora Merino (120m per 50g ball)
- 1 x 50g ball shade 41 Linen (A)
- 1 x 50g ball 072 Giggle Pink (B)
- 1 x 50g ball 45 Chilli (C)
- 1 set 4mm double-pointed needles

Measurements

10in (25cm) wide x 15in (38cm) to top

Tension

20 sts x 24 rows to 4in (10cm) over st st using 4mm needles.

Special techniques

- Circular knitting
- Cover is worked using the Fair Isle method, weaving spare yarn at back of work

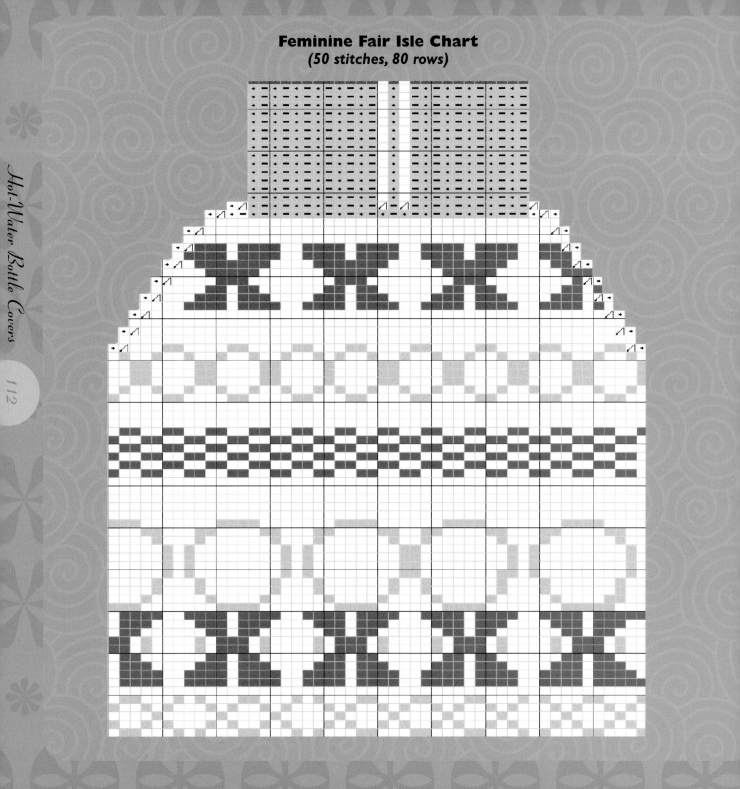

Feminine Fair Isle Chart
(50 stitches, 80 rows)

Back and front

Using 4mm needles and A, cast on
100 sts.
Place marker before st 1 and st 50.
Foll chart until row 47 has been
completed.

Chart key

✛	Knit
▬	Purl
◸	Decrease by working 2 sts tog

Top shaping

Follow chart to shape top of cover OR
follow these instructions:

Round 48: P1, ssk to dec, work 44 sts
in patt, k2 tog to dec, p2, ssk, work 44
sts in patt, k2tog, p1 (96 sts).

Next round: Work straight without
dec, foll patt as set.

Cont as set, dec 4 sts on every alt
round (2 sts on each side of cover) and
p2 between decs, until row 62 of chart
has been completed (68 sts).

Round 63: Work as a dec round
(64 sts).

Round 64: Work in rib, dec 16 sts
evenly across the round (8 sts each side)
by working k2tog or p2tog (48 sts).
Work 15 rows k1, p1 rib using B.
Cast off loosely using C.

Making up

Dry press cover.
Join part of lower seam, insert bottle,
then complete seam using backstitch.

This sumptuously soft cover is worked in a Fair Isle pattern in strong, masculine colours to remind him of his favourite sweater.

Macho Fair Isle

Materials
- Sublime Angora Merino DK (120m per 50g ball)
- 2 x 50g balls shade 46
- 1 x 50g ball shade 47
- 1 x 50g ball shade 47
- A pair of 4mm (UK8:US6) needles
- A pair 3.75mm (UK9:US5) needles
- 3 medium buttons

Tension
22 sts x 28 rows to 4in (10cm) over stocking stitch using 4mm needles

Measurements
10in (25cm wide x 15in (38cm) to top

Special techniques
- The front of the cover is worked in Fair Isle, carrying the yarn across the back of work, and the back is in stocking stitch

Note: if you want to work the whole cover in fairisle, follow instructions for fairisle back

Front

Using 4mm needles and A, cast on 28 sts and work in st st throughout.

Next row (RS): K to end.

Next row: Foll chart from row 2, and at the same time cast on 4 sts at the beg of the next 4 rows.

Inc 1 st at each end of next 3 rows.

Work straight, following chart, until row 70 has been worked, ending with RS facing for next row.

Still following chart, dec 1 st at each end of next 3 rows.

Cast off 4 sts at the beg of next 4 rows.

Next row: P, inc 1 st at centre of row (29 sts).

Leave rem sts on a spare length of yarn.

Plain back

Using 4mm needles and A, cast on 28 sts and work in st st throughout.

Next row (RS): K to end.

Cast on 4 sts at beg of next 4 rows.

Inc 1 st at each end of next 3 rows (50 sts).

Work straight for a further 34 rows ending with RS facing for next row.

**Change to 3.75mm needles

Row 1: K2, *p2, k2; rep from * to end.

Row 2: P2, *k2, p2; rep from * to end.

Rep last 2 rows 3 more times (8 rows).

Cast off in rib.

Upper back (plain)

Using 3.75mm needles and A, cast on 50 sts.

Work 3 rows rib as for lower back.

Next row (buttonhole): Rib 5, *cast off 2 sts, rib 16; rep from * once more, cast off 2 sts, rib to end.

Next row: Work as for row 1 of lower back, casting on 2 sts over those cast off on previous row.

Rib a further 3 rows, ending with RS facing for next row.

Change to 4mm needles. ******

Work straight for 20 rows ending with RS facing for next row.

Dec 1 st at each end of next 3 rows.

Cast off 4 sts at beg next 4 rows.

Next row: P all sts, inc1 in centre of row (29 sts).

Leave sts on needle.

Rib collar

Change to 3.75mm needles to work rib.

Next row (RS): Still using A, *k2, p2; rep from * to last st, k1 but do not turn. Transfer sts from spare yarn to left needle; k1, *p2, k2; rep from * to end.

Next row (WS): *p2, k2; rep from * to last 2 sts, p2.

Row 2: *k2, p2, rep from * to last 2 sts, k2.

Rep last 2 rows until rib measures 7¼ in (18.5cm), ending with row 1.

Cast off in rib.

Rib collar

Work as for option 1.

Making up

Press pieces lightly foll instructions on ball band.

Join lower back seam to front lower back, then upper front and back overlapping buttonhole row to button band.

Attach buttons to correspond with buttonholes.

Join polo neck, reversing seams halfway to allow collar to be folded.

Fair Isle back

Work as for front until row 42 of chart has been worked.

Next row (RS): Using A only, work as for front from ** to ** (this includes beg of patt for upper back).

Upper back

Beg with row 51 of chart (inc this row), cont until row 70 has been worked, ending with RS facing for next row.

Still following chart, dec1 at each end of next 3 rows.

Cast off 4 sts at beg of next 4 rows.

Next row: P all sts, inc1 at centre of row (29 sts).

Leave sts on needle.

Macho Fair Isle Chart
(52 stitches, 75 rows)

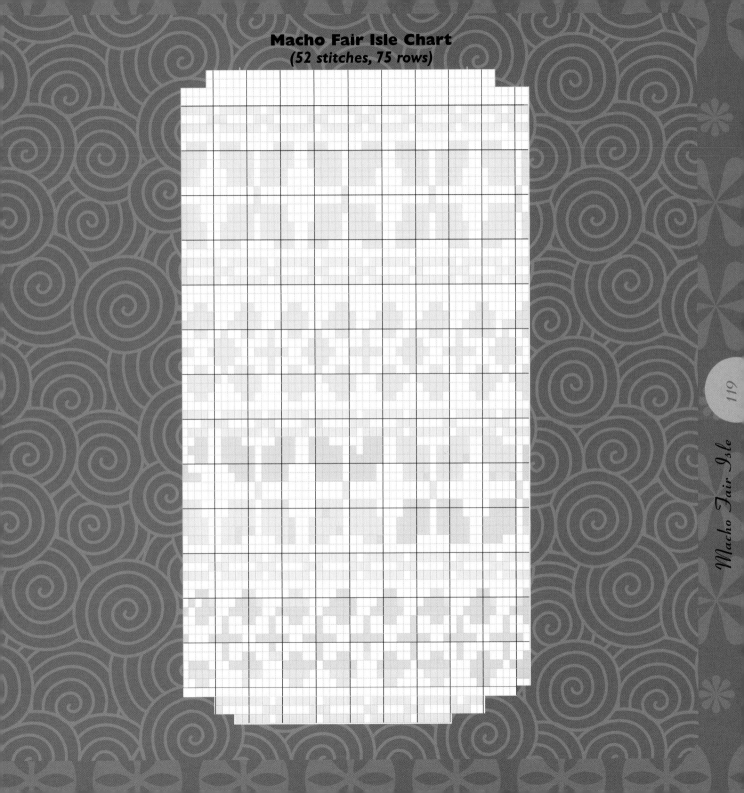

This simple but stunning cover in unusual shades
was inspired by rows of vines in a Tuscan vineyard.
The diagonal pattern is easy but effective.

Diagonal Stripe

Materials

- Rowan Kid Classic (140m per 50g ball)
- 1 x 50g ball 854 Tea Rose (A)
- 1 x 50g ball Aubergine 852 (B)
- 1 x 50g ball 845 Green (C)
- A pair of 4mm (UK8:US9) needles
- A pair of 5mm (UK6:US8) needles
- 4.50mm (UK7:US7) crochet hook
- Ready-made template or card to make pompons

Measurements

9in (23cm) wide x 14½in (37cm) long including
top gathering

Tension

20 sts and 24 rows to 4in (10cm) over st st using
5mm needles

Special techniques

- Pompons (see below)
- yrn = yarn round needle
- Intarsia method = use separate small balls of yarn
  for each block of colour, twisting yarns securely at back
  of work to avoid gaps

Front

Using C and 4mm needles, cast on 45 sts and foll chart 1, working in st st and using the intarsia method.

Row 1 (RS): K15C, k15B, k15A.

Next row: Foll chart from row 2 for 4 rows.

Change to 5mm needles and work until row 72 has been completed, ending with RS facing for next row.

Next row (eyelets): Keeping the stripe sequence as set, *k2, yrn, k2tog, k6; rep from * to last 3 sts, yrn, k2tog, k1.

Foll chart until row 88 has been worked, ending with RS facing for next row.

Change to 4mm needles.

Using C only, work 3 rows g-st (every row knit).

Cast off k-wise.

Back

Using C and 5mm needles, cast on 45 sts.

Change to A.

Next row (RS): K15A, k15B, k15C.

Foll chart 2 from row 2, working the diagonal stripes as marked, for 4 rows.

Change to 5mm needles and work until row 72 has been completed, ending with RS facing for next row.

Work eyelet row as for front.

Cont to foll chart until row 88 has been worked.

Next row

Change to 4mm needles and work edging as for front.

Cast off knitwise.

Making up

Pin out the pieces and damp press.

Using mattress st, join sides and bottom edge.

Drawstring

Using 4.50mm crochet hook and 2 strands of B make a chain 26in (66cm) long, leaving approx 4in (10cm) at each end of drawstring to tie on pompons. Thread drawstring through eyelets, starting and ending at centre front of cover.

Note: If you cannot crochet, make a cord by finger knitting or plaiting.

Pompons (make 2)

Use a ready-made template or make a template from two pieces of card, cut into a 2in (5cm) circles with smaller circles cut in the centre of each.

Using A and C, wrap yarn round template until it is tightly packed.

Using a pair of narrow-pointed scissors, cut between the 2 cards.

Tie the loose ends of the cord tightly into centre of pompons.

Ease off both pieces of card and fluff up pompons.

Trim edges to form a smooth ball.

Diagonal Stripe Chart (front)
(45 stitches, 90 rows)

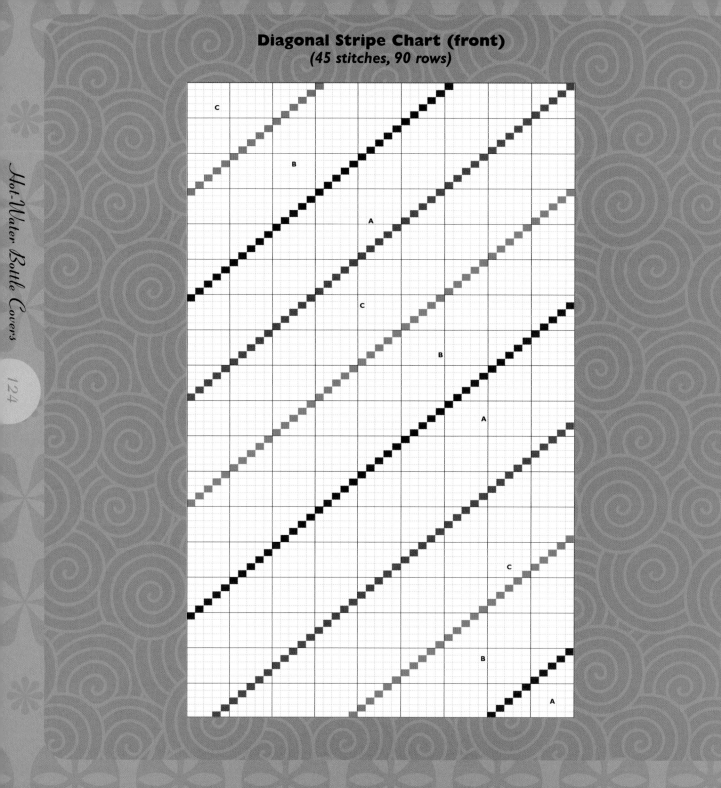

Diagonal Stripe Chart (back)
(45 stitches, 90 rows)

Diagonal Stripe

Inspired by children's drawings, this cover has a bus on one side
and a boat on the other – perfect for any little boy.

Buses and Boats

Materials

- Filatura di Crosa Zara DK (136yds/125m per 50g ball)
- 2 x 50g balls shade 1396 cream (A)
- 1 x 50g ball shade 1466 red (B)
- 1 x 50g ball shade 430 blue (C)
- 1 ball shade 1410 black (D)
- A pair of 3.75mm (UK9:US5) needles
- A pair of 3.25mm (UK10:US3) needles

Measurements

9in (23cm) wide × 14½in (37cm) total length

Tension

23 sts and 31 rows to 10cm (4in) over st st using
3.75mm needles

Special techniques

- Cover is worked in st st using the Intarsia method,
  using separate balls of yarn for each block of colour

Top shaping

Dec1 at each end of next row.

Work 1 row.

Dec1 at each end of next 2 rows.

Work 1 row.

Cast off 3 sts at beg of next 2 rows, ending with WS facing for next row (38 sts).

Leave rem sts on spare length of yarn.

Back

Using 3.75mm needles and A, cast on 26 sts.

Work shaping as for font but foll chart for back until row 87 has been worked, ending with WS facing for next row.

Change to 3.25mm needles and using A only, p across sts on needle, transfer sts from spare length of yarn to left needle p across (76 sts).

Rib collar

Next row: *k1, p1; rep from * to end.

Rep this row until rib measures 15½in (14cm).

Change to C and cont as set until rib measures 6in (15.5cm) in total ending with WS of collar facing.

Cast off in rib.

Front

Using 3.75mm needles and A, cast on 26 sts.

Row 1 (RS): K all sts.

Cast on 4 sts at beg of next 2 rows.

Cast on 3 sts at beg of next 2 rows.

Cast on 2 sts at beg of next 2 rows.

Inc 1 st at each end of next 3 rows.

Follow chart from row 11 until row 80 has been worked.

Making up

Pin out and damp press following directions on ball band.

Join side and bottom seams.

Join rib collar halfway, reversing seam to allow it to be folded over.

Place bottle in cover via the wide polo neck.

Buses and Boats
(52 stitches, 87 rows)

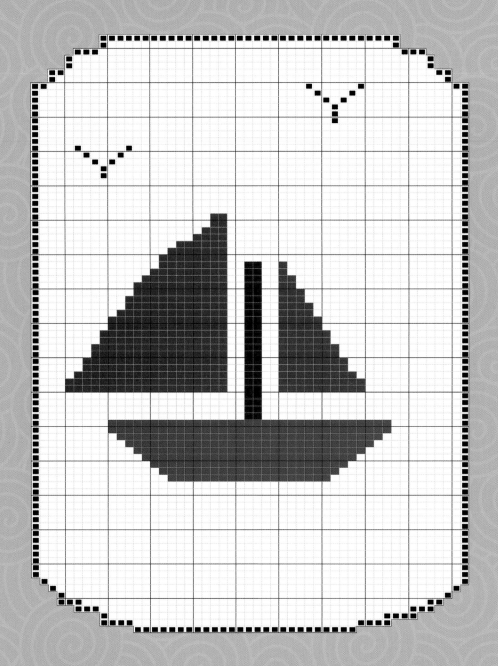

Buses and Boats
(52 stitches, 87 rows)

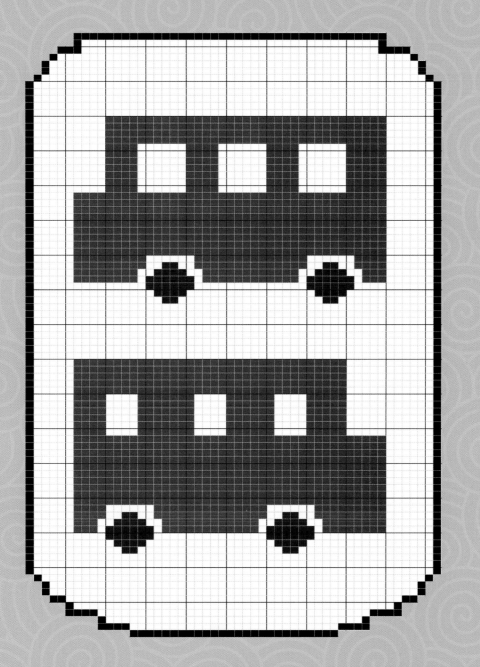

A stunning combination of contrasting shades makes a really modern cover, and the simple circle design is great fun to knit.

Stunning Circles

Materials

- Lana Grossa Pashmina (135yds/124m per 50g ball)
- 2 x 50g balls shade 18 green (A)
- 1 x 50g ball shade 10 maroon (B)
- 1 x 50g ball shade 14 grey (C)
- A pair of 3.25mm (UK10:US3) needles
- A pair of 4mm (UK8:US6) needles
- 3 medium buttons

Measurements

9in (23cm) wide x 14in (35.5cm) total length

Tension

24 sts x 30 rows to 4in (10cm) over st st using 4mm needles

Special techniques

- Cover is worked in st st using the Intarsia method, changing colours where indicated and using separate balls of yarn for each block of colour.

Front

Using 4mm needles and A cast on 28 sts.
*K 1 row (RS facing).
Cast on 4 sts at beg of next 4 rows.
P 1 row.
Inc1 at each end of next and foll alt row.
P 1 row.

Next row (RS): Inc1 at each end of
row and *at the same time* beg to foll
chart from row 11 * to row 78
(inclusive).

Top shaping

Dec1 at each end of next 3 rows.
Work 1 row without dec.
Cast off 4 sts at beg of next 4 rows,
ending with RS facing for next row
(28 sts).
Change to 3.25mm needles.

Next row: K all sts.
Rep last row until g-st border measures
6¼in (16cm), ending with RS facing for
next row.
Turn chart upside-down, as this makes it
easier to read.
Change to 4mm needles and foll chart
down from row 86, working top back
shaping at the same time.

Top back shaping

Knit 1 row
Cast on 4 sts at beg of next 4 rows.
Purl 1 row.
Inc1 at each each end of next 3 rows.
Now follow chart to row 52 (inclusive)
reversing the colours of the circles.
Change to 3.25mm needles

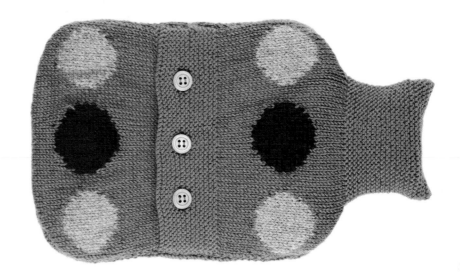

Next row (buttonhole band): K all
sts. Repeat last row until g-st measures
1in (2.5cm).

Next row (buttonhole): *k11, cast off
next 2 sts; rep from * twice more, k to
end.

Next row: K all sts, casting on 2 sts over
those cast off on previous row.
Work in g-st until band measures 2in
(5cm).
Cast off k-wise.

Lower back

Using 4mm needles and M, cast on
28 sts.
Foll chart until row 36 has been worked,
reversing colours for circles and at the
same time foll shaping for lower front
from * to * .
Change to 3.25mm needles

Next row: K all sts.
Rep last row until band measures the
same as band on top back.
Cast off k-wise.

Making up

Join lower back to lower front sides and
bottom edge.
Fold over g-st band half-way to form
upper back and sew in place, overlapping
the buttonhole and button bands.
Attach buttons to correspond with
buttonholes.

Stunning Circles
(50 stitches, 86 rows)

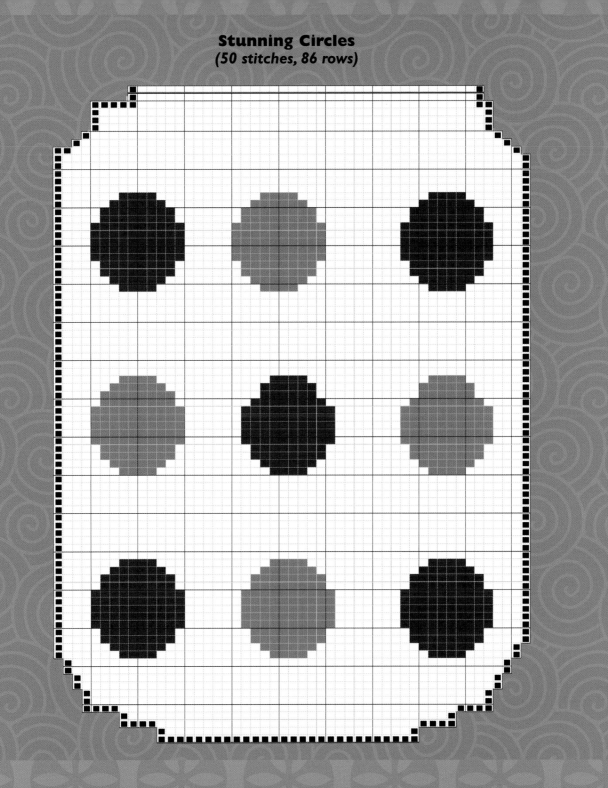

A naked hot-water bottle!

Techniques

How to make your hot-water bottle decent

Measurements

An average hot water bottle is about 8in (20.3cm) wide and 13in (33cm) long. A child-size bottle is about 5in (12.5cm) wide and 8½in (21.5cm) long. If your bottle is slightly wider than this, the patterns should still fit as the work is stretchy. If it is slightly longer, you may need to adjust the length by working a few extra rows. Try the cover on the bottle as you work, or hold the pattern piece against the bottle to make sure that you are happy before casting off. If you do adjust the length, make sure you add rows to both sides of the pattern.

Tension

Tension is important as just a slight difference can have a noticeable effect on the size of the finished cover. It is a good idea to start a habit that will save a lot of time in the end: work a swatch using the chosen yarn and needles. These can be labelled and filed for future reference. The tension required is given at the beginning of each pattern.

Needles

Most of the hot water bottle covers in this book are worked back and forth on standard knitting needles. A few are worked in the round on double-pointed or circular needles.

Yarn

Hot water bottle covers may be made in a huge variety of yarns, from luxurious cashmere or alpaca to smooth cotton. If you are allergic to wool, choose one of the excellent synthetic yarns on the market, or opt for cotton or silk.

Substituting yarn

It is relatively simple to substitute different yarns for any of the projects in this book, but remember to check your tension. One way to substitute yarn is to work out how many wraps per inch (wpi) the yarn produces. Do this by winding it closely, in a single layer, round a rule or similar object and counting how many 'wraps' to an inch (2.5cm) it produces. For a successful result, pick a yarn that produces twice, or a little more than twice, the number of wraps per inch (or slightly more) as there are stitches per inch in the tension swatch.

Tension required	Use yarn with this no. of WPI
8 sts per in (4-ply/fingering)	16–18 wpi
6.5 sts per in (DK/sport)	13–14 wpi
5.5 sts per in (chunky/worsted)	11–12 wpi

Knit stitch

1. Hold the needle with the cast-on stitches in your left hand. Place the tip of the empty right-hand needle into the first stitch. Wrap the yarn around as for casting on.

2. Pull the yarn through the needle to create a new loop.

3. Slip the new stitch on to the right-hand needle.

Continue in the same way for each stitch on the left-hand needle.

To start a new row, exchange the needles so that the left needle is full once again and repeat instructions.

Purl stitch

1 Hold the yarn to the front of the work as shown.

2 Place the right needle into the first stitch from front to back. Wrap the yarn around right needle in an anti-clockwise direction as shown.

3 Bring the needle down and back through the stitch, and pull through.

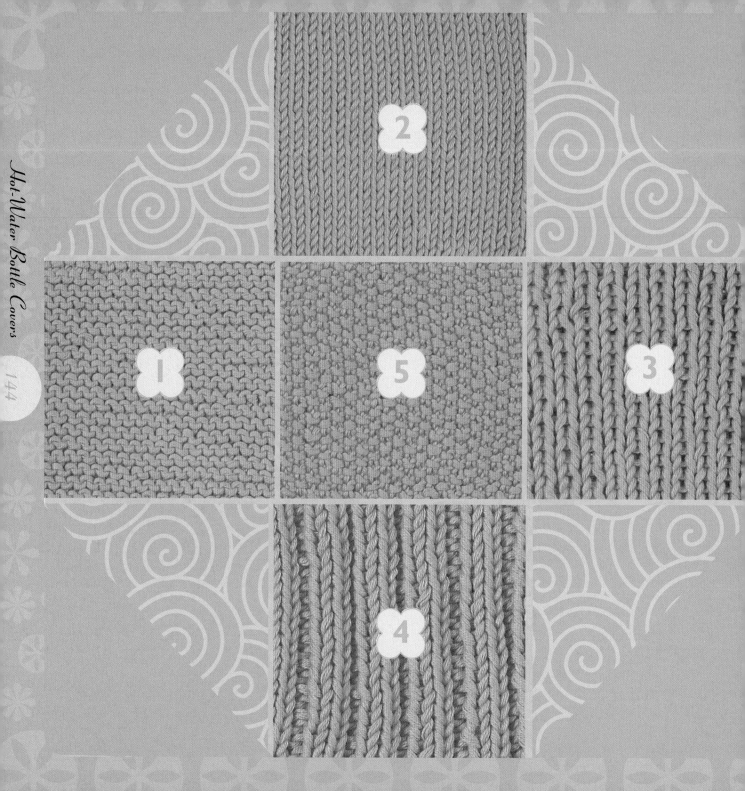

Types of stitches

1 Garter stitch

Knit every row.
In the round, knit 1 row, purl 1 row.

2 Stocking stitch

Knit RS rows; purl WS rows.
In the round, knit every row.

3 Single rib

With an even number of stitches:
Row 1: *k1, p1* rep to end.
Rep for each row.
With an odd number of stitches:
Row 1: *k1, p1, rep from * to last stitch, k1.
Row 2: *p1, k1, rep from * to last stitch, p1.

4 Double rib

Row 1: *k2, p2, rep from * to end.
Rep for each row.

5 Moss stitch

Starting with an even number of stitches:
Row 1: (K1, P1) to end.
Row 2: (P1, K1) to end.
Rep rows 1 and 2 to form pattern.
Starting with an odd number of stitches:
Row 1: *K1, P1, rep from * to last st, K1.
Rep to form pattern.

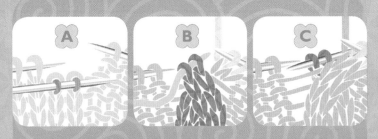

6 Cable stitch

These decorative stitches are easy to work using a cable needle. Stitches are held on the cable needle, then worked later to create twists. The example shows 2 sts being cabled, but this method can be used to cable any number of stitches.

Cable 2F

A Slip the next 2 sts on to a cable needle and hold in front of work.

B Knit the next 2 sts from the left needle, then k2 from the cable needle.

Cable 2B

C Slip 2 sts on to a cable needle and hold at back of work; k2 from left needle, then k2 from cable needle.

Techniques

Working in the round

Double-pointed needles
These usually come in sets of four or five.

1 Reserve one needle to work with and space the cast-on stitches out evenly on the remaining needles.

2 When the first set of stitches has been worked, the reserved needle will take the place of the first needle and so on. Once mastered, the technique is very effective. Pull the yarn taut between each needle to avoid gaps in your work.

Circular needle
This comprises two needles joined with plastic cable, and is used to work in rounds. Any size of needle may be used with any number of stitches – its length does not have to match the circumference of the work. First, mark the beginning of the round with thread, or use the cast-on tail as a reminder. About a third of the way round the needle, pull a loop of cable from between two stitches until they close to form a ring. Work up to the loop, then slide the next section of stitches up to the point of the needle, leaving a loop as before. As work progresses it should be possible to move more stitches at a time. Choose a slightly different place on each round to prevent stretched stitches. If adding patterns, it is particularly important to note where the round begins. If the loop of cable is troublesome, slip it over the wrist as you work.

Joining seams

Stocking stitch joins

The edges of stocking stitch tend to curl so it may be tricky to join. The best way to join is to use mattress stitch to pick up the bars between the columns of stitches.

Working up or down as preferred, secure yarn to one of the pieces you wish to join. Place the edges of the work together and pick up a bar from one side, then the corresponding bar from the opposite side. Repeat. Do not pull the stitches at first as you will not be able to see what you are doing. After a few stitches, pull gently on the yarn, and the edges will come together in a seam that is almost invisible. Take care to stay in the same column all the way.

Garter stitch joins

It is easy to join garter stitch as it has a firm edge and lies flat. Place the edges of the work together, right side up, and check how the stitches line up. Pick up the bottom loops of the stitches on one side of the work and the top loops from the other. After a few stitches, pull the yarn gently; the stitches should lock together and lie completely flat. The inside of the join should look the same as the outside.

Kitchener stitch/ Kitchener grafting

This is a method of grafting stitches invisibly together. To begin, divide the stitches you wish to join evenly between two double-pointed needles. Hold both needles parallel in your left hand, so the working yarn is to your right and is coming off the first stitch on the back needle. Cut the working yarn to a reasonable working length.

- Using a third needle, **purl** the first stitch on the **front** needle.
- Drop the stitch off the left front needle, and pull the yarn all the way through the dropped stitch so that there is no longer a stitch on the right (working) needle.
- **Knit** the next stitch on the **front** needle, but this time leave the stitch on the left front needle and pull the yarn all the way through as before.
- **Knit** the first stitch on the **back** needle.
- Drop the stitch off the left back needle and pull the yarn all the way through.
- **Purl** the next stitch on the **back** needle.
- **Leave** this stitch on the left back needle and pull the yarn all the way through.

Repeat as set until two stitches remain, then k2tog and pull the yarn all the way through. Thread on a tapestry needle. Bring to the inside of work and weave in ends, tacking down the last loops as necessary for a neat finish.

1 **Fair Isle designs**

Where two colours are used in one row do not leave long loops at the back of the work. When a colour is used over just one or two stitches, leave the other colour at the back of your work and pick it up when it is required. If either yarn needs to be taken across a space of more than three stitches, twist both yarns together every two or three stitches.

2 To do this is to cross one yarn from top to bottom at the first twist and from bottom to top at the next twist. This will help to stop yarns from tangling. Take care not to pull the yarns too tightly or it will gather your work and the tension may be too tight.

Colour knitting

Intarsia designs

These are designs worked using blocks of colour. Where several colours are used you can combine Fair Isle and intarsia techniques by dropping some colours and carrying others.

Use a separate ball of yarn for each block, and twist the yarns together each time you change colour to prevent holes forming between the blocks. Remember not to pull the yarns too tightly across the back of the work.

Reading charts

Most charts are shown in squares, with a square representing one stitch. Charts are usually marked in sections of ten stitches to make counting easier.

Stocking stitch

When working in stocking stitch on straight needles, read the chart from right to left on knit (RS) rows and from left to right on purl (WS) rows. Check carefully after every purl row to make sure pattern stitches are in the right position.

In the round

If you work a chart in the round, you will always be working from right to left, so you will always be able to see how the pictures or letters are forming. What you see on your work should correspond exactly with the chart.

<!-- decorative hot water bottle cover image -->

Increases

There are many different ways to increase stitches, and knitters tend to stick with what they prefer. As with decreases, use the same method of increasing throughout a garment to ensure the best effect.

Simple increase

The easiest way to increase is by working twice into a stitch. To do this knitwise, simply knit the stitch as normal but do not remove the loop from the left-hand needle. Wrap the yarn over the needle again and knit into the back of the stitch before removing the loop from the left-hand needle.

M1R = make one stitch slanting to the right

Find the horizontal connecting yarn between the needles. Using the left needle, pick up the connecting yarn **from the back to the front** and leave this 'raised bar' on the left needle. Work the raised bar by knitting (RS row) or purling (WS row) as appropriate.

M1L = make one stitch slanting to the left

Find the horizontal connecting yarn between the needles. Using the left needle, pick up the connecting yarn **from the front to the back** and leave this 'raised bar' on the left needle. Then either knit the raised bar through the back of the loop (RS row) or purl the raised bar (WS row).

Decreases

Methods of decreasing are interchangeable, so choose the one you prefer, but remember to use it consistently for a neat overall appearance.

Use a left-slanting decrease at the beginning of a needle and the right-slanting decrease at the end of a needle.

Left-slanting decreases

Ssk

Slip 2 sts knitwise, return sts to left needle, place the needle into the back of the yarn loops, and knit them together.

ssk (variation)

Slip 1st knitwise, then 1 st purlwise, return the sts to the left needle, then knit them together through the back of loops.

Ssp

Slip 2 sts knitwise, return the sts to the left needle, then purl them together through the back of the loops.

Skpo

Slip 1 st knitwise, k1, then pass the slipped stitch over the knitted st.

K2tog tbl

Knit two stitches together through the back of the yarn loops

Right-slanting decreases

K2tog

Knit two stitches together through the front of the loops.

Conversions

Needle sizes

UK	Metric	US
14	2mm	0
13	2.5mm	1
12	2.75mm	2
11	3mm	–
10	3.25mm	3
–	3.5mm	4
9	3.75mm	5
8	4mm	6
7	4.5mm	7
6	5mm	8
5	5.5mm	9
4	6mm	10
3	6.5mm	10.5
2	7mm	10.5
1	7.5mm	11
0	8mm	11
00	9mm	13
000	10mm	15

UK/US Yarn Weights

UK	US
2–ply	Lace
3–ply	Fingering
4–ply	Sport
Double knitting	Light worsted
Aran	Fisherman/Worsted
Chunky	Bulky
Super chunky	Extra bulky

Abbreviations

approx	approximately
cont	continue
cm	centimetres
d g-st	double garter stitch (2 rounds p, 2 rounds k)
DK	double knitting
foll	following
inc	increase by working twice into stitch
in(s)	inch(es)
k	knit
k-wise	with needles positioned as for working a knit stitch
k2tog	knit two stitches together
MIL	make 1 stitch slanting to the left
MIR	make 1 st slanting to the right
p	purl
p2tog	purl two stitches together
p-wise	with needles positioned as for working a purl stitch
rem	remaining
rep	repeat
RS	right side of work
skpo	slip one, knit one, pass slipped stitch over
ss	slip stitch
ssk	slip one stitch knitwise, then slip 1 st purlwise, then knit the two stitches together through the back of the lookps
ssp	slip one stitch k-wise, slip one stitch p-wise, then purl sts tog
st(s)	stitch(es)
*	work instructions following * then repeat as directed
( )	repeat instructions inside brackets as directed
WS	wrong side of work

The author and GMC Publications would like to thank:

Jenny Shore for her help with knitting the covers and writing patterns, Christian Funnell and Diana Mothersole for the loan of their beautiful homes in East Sussex and Brighton and numerous photographic props, and various companies, including Rowan Yarns, for supplying some of the raw materials.

Remembered with affection is Chrissie Day's beloved father-in-law Derek H. Day, who died during the making of this book. Jenny also lost her much-loved father Walter Shore.

The yarns featured in this book are available from online stores or from well-stocked yarn shops.

Chrissie Day is happy to answer queries from readers. For knitting tips and enquiries about any of the patterns in this book visit her website at: **www.chrissieday.co.uk**

I cannot remember a time before knitting,
a time when yarn did not run through my fingers and feature in my life.
I was first recorded knitting at the age of four, along with my darling grandmother
who taught me all she knew about fibres. I knitted through my childhood and teenage
years, gaining a Guides' badge; through long hours of night duty as a student nurse;
in many countries while travelling; through lonely evenings and sad times and through
happy times and my children's childhoods. If stitches were tears I might have knitted
an ocean by now, but just as much of my work has soft memories of golden times
worked into every stitch.

After my introduction to felt-making, I began making things bigger simply to felt them
down to size. Patterns were redefined and yarn trials carried out; I began to push
boundaries by combining materials and techniques in unusual ways. I love
experimenting and adding in other fibres, and choosing colours and yarns is always a
challenge. Knitting is addictive yet calming, helping me to be at one with the ups and
downs of life. Let it into your life and enjoy the journey.

My inspiration comes from nature and my garden in every season, as well as
architecture that arrests my attention as I travel, from a Greek door with peeling paint
to Madrid's prize-winning new airport. I hope you enjoy making these designs as
much as I enjoyed creating them.

Chrissie Day

Index

Contact us for a complete catalogue, or visit our website:
GMC Publications Ltd, 166 High Street, Lewes, East Sussex BN7 1XU, United Kingdom
Tel: +44 (0)1273 488005 Fax: +44 (0)1273 402866
www.gmcbooks.com